SOUTH-EAST ASIA

D1596025

ON

PHILIPPINES

MINDANAO

IRIAN JAYA

E   S   I   A

BOK

SUMBA

IMAGES OF ASIA

Rice in South-East Asia

Titles in the series

Rice in South-East Asia

Cultures and Landscapes

JACQUELINE M. PIPER

KUALA LUMPUR
OXFORD UNIVERSITY PRESS
OXFORD SINGAPORE NEW YORK
1993

Oxford University Press

Oxford New York Toronto
Delhi Bombay Calcutta Madras Karachi
Kuala Lumpur Singapore Hong Kong Tokyo
Nairobi Dar es Salaam Cape Town
Melbourne Auckland Madrid

and associated companies in
Berlin Ibadan

Oxford is a trade mark of Oxford University Press

Published in the United States
by Oxford University Press, New York

British Library Cataloguing in Publication Data
Data available

Library of Congress Cataloging-in-Publication Data

Piper, Jacqueline M.
Rice in South-East Asia: cultures and landscapes/Jacqueline M. Piper.
p. cm.—(Images of Asia)
Includes bibliographical references and index.
ISBN 9676530387:
1. Rice—Asia, Southeastern—Folklore. 2. Rice—Social aspects—Asia, Southeastern.
3. Man—Influence on nature—Asia, Southeastern. 4. Landscape assessment—Asia,
Southeastern. 5. Material culture—Asia, Southeastern. 6. Asia, Southeastern—Social life
and customs. I. Title. II. Series.
GR308.P56 1993
398'. 355—dc20
93-20669
CIP

Typeset by Indah Photosetting Centre Sdn. Bhd., Malaysia
Printed by Kim Hup Lee Printing Co. Pte. Ltd., Singapore
Published by Oxford University Press,
19–25, Jalan Kuchai Lama, 58200 Kuala Lumpur, Malaysia

For Molly and Anne

Preface

THIS is neither a cookbook nor a farmer's guide. Instead, it is concerned with the role of rice in the lives of the peoples of South-East Asia—how it shapes the landscapes they see around them, how it contributes to the ordering of their lives.

The countries of South-East Asia are agriculture-based: most of the people are involved in farming, and with a few industrialized exceptions, the greater part of each national economy hinges on agriculture. And it is, of course, rice that is the staple product of agriculture, the principal sustenance of the region's peoples.

The study of rice—how it is grown and its place in communities and societies—gives us a keyhole through which we can gain insight into the wealth of South-East Asian cultures. Many crop plants have folk-tales and beliefs associated with them, but it is those that have for the longest time sustained mankind, such as rice and bananas, that have the richest attendant folklore. Many of these stories are reproduced here.

In order to simplify the immense variety of rice production in South-East Asia and to relate it to the environments within the region, I have first taken three major landscapes (effectively, ecosystems) in which rice is grown: the mountain forests, the flood plains, and the hill terraces. Then, for each of these landscapes, some examples of popular beliefs and practices are presented. Many common themes exist: the place of the gods in giving rice to man, the holiness of rice, and the use of rice to express simple realities of human life, such as the relationship between spouses.

Chapter 1 introduces rice as a crop and as a food; it then describes the landscapes in which it is grown and the diversity of rice. Chapter 2 discusses the way rice was developed and how it spread across not only South-East Asia, but the globe. Major social consequences seem to have stemmed from the adoption of rice as a principal food and from the use of irrigation. Other uses of rice—for wine, ceremonial, and industry—are mentioned, including the connection with arts and crafts. Chapters 3, 4, and 5 look at each of three types of land where rice is the main crop and describe how the people living in these lands grow their rice, as well as something of their customs. Chapter 4 includes a section on the water-buffalo in South-East Asia as the animal has long been important in rice production and, in consequence, in local folk-lore.

Although references to man's interactions with the spirit world are scattered throughout the text, more folk-stories and practices are grouped together in Chapter 6. A book this size cannot be comprehensive but what I hope it will communicate is something of the wealth of culture associated with this ancient and diverse cereal crop. Rice has shaped not only the environment in which the peoples of South-East Asia live, but also the pattern of their lives.

I have received much help with obtaining the illustrations for this book. These are listed in full in the Acknowledgements, but I should particularly like to thank David Kinnersley, Denis Robinson, Ric Vokes, and David Warrell, who took photographs especially for this project, and Ben Piper for his help.

Wolfson College, Oxford   JACQUELINE M. PIPER
January 1993

Acknowledgements

I should like to thank the following individuals and institutions for their help in providing illustrations for this book:

British Library, London (Plate 3)
A. A. M. Djelantik, Walter Spies Foundation, Bali (Colour Plate 8)
Ghulam-Sarwar Yousof (Colour Plate 20)
Irwin Hersey (Colour Plate 23)
International Rice Research Institute, Manila (Plates 11 and 18 and Colour Plates 2 and 16)
David Kinnersley (Plate 22)
Oriental Hotel, Bangkok (Plate 19)
Denis Robinson (Plates 4, 9, and 10 and Colour Plates 4, 6, and 7)
Royal Thai Embassy, London (Plates 17 and 21 and Colour Plates 13 and 24)
Sarawak Museum, Kuching (Plates 6 and 8 and Colour Plates 3 and 5)
Grace Selvanayagam (Plates 5 and 7)
David Stuart-Fox and Francine Brinkgreve (Colour Plates 18 and 19)
Chaiyuth Sukhsri (Colour Plate 12)
Vinson Sutlive (Plates 1, 12, and 13)
Tropenmuseum, Amsterdam (Plate 14)
Ric Vokes (Colour Plates 10, 11, 14, and 21)
David Warrell (Colour Plates 15 and 22)
Roxanna Waterson (Plates 20 and 23 and Colour Plate 9)

Contents

1
Introduction

The Importance of Rice

'WHERE the curry is good, the rice is half-cooked; when the rice is good, the curry is half-cooked' runs a world-weary Malay proverb. Another warns: 'Without rice, there is nothing doing.' This is undeniably true in South-East Asia where rice is the staple food. In South-East Asian languages, 'to eat' and 'to eat rice' are often synonymous (for example, *tarn kao* in Thai, *ngajengang* in Balinese). To Thai villagers, man's body itself is rice and eating rice renews the body directly; mothers' milk is blood purified to the whiteness of rice.

Rice has been cultivated in South-East Asia for 7,000 years and more, so cultures and cultivation are interwoven with each other. The farming calendar provides the warp or the structure of the year, whilst ceremonies, beliefs, and customs provide the weft, building up the patterns of the brightly coloured cloth that is life in South-East Asia.

Whilst it is the only sustenance of the poor in hard times, rice is also the basis of almost all South-East Asian cultures and civilizations. Its adaptability to very different environments has made farming possible in areas where no other crop could be grown so successfully—from swampy valleys and deltas to hot, dry land above the floods and even in the mountain forests. Thus, rice can be said to be responsible for South-East Asia's high population: if rice had not replaced the millets and other staple crops that preceded it, far fewer people could have been supported by agriculture.

Whether it is rice or wheat that nourishes more of the world's human population is an open question, but more than half of the world's population now lives in Asia. Of that number, two-thirds are dependent on farming and live on the flood plains and deltas of the great rivers of East and South-East Asia, such as the Huang Ho,

1

the Yangtze, the Red River, the Mekong, the Chao Phraya, and the Irrawaddy. Further west, rice is also an important staple of the rivers and deltas of the Indian subcontinent.

Population growth and rice production go hand in hand. Asia as a whole, an arc from Korea to Pakistan, is the most densely populated region in the world, with only 24 per cent of the world's cultivated area but 56 per cent of its population. Rice is not, of course, the only staple crop grown in this region, but it is certainly the major one.

Landscapes and Farming

Rice is not a crop which blends into the landscape. Rather, cultivation of rice sculpts the landscape to the crop's needs. In the hill forests, an undistinguished landscape arises where slash-and-burn or shifting cultivation is practised. Shifting cultivators clear small patches in the forest for a few short years of cropping. If too frequently repeated, shifting cultivation may lead to an impoverished plant cover of small trees and bush. Plate 1 shows an Iban shifting cultivator transporting rice from the fields back to his longhouse—the basket and sacks may weigh up to 80 kilograms.

Paddy or wet-land rice farming, on the other hand, is carried out in tranquil, majestic landscapes fashioned in every detail by the hand of man, landscapes that are totally unnatural but immensely serene. Rice dominates the mouths of the river valleys of Asia: the deltas and flood plains of the Mekong, the Chao Phraya, the Yangtze, the Ganges, the Irrawaddy, and the Hongshui (Pearl) Rivers. The woodlands and bamboo groves that once grew in these well-watered and fertile plains have been felled or burned and the great expanses have been ploughed flat. Fruit trees and palms, especially coconuts and sugar palms, are planted to help shore up the bunds between the paddies, thus helping to control the flow of water. Rice and water, palms and fruit trees, stretching from horizon to horizon, make up the landscape that the peoples of rural Asia have known for centuries.

Terraces are found in some countries, away from the flood plain and into the hills. The terraces of the Ifugao of the Philippines and

2

the Igorot of Malaysia are some of the best known but terraces also clothe hillsides in Sri Lanka, Java, Thailand, and Nepal. The terrace is a way of making it possible to use almost precipitous slopes for agriculture. A retaining wall is built of stones or earth and secured with planted trees and bushes which bind the wall with their roots. The land behind the wall, which may be a very small area, is levelled and ploughed. Water is diverted into it from a stream and then drained out to irrigate lower terraces. The flow of water must be carefully controlled so as not to wash out the retaining wall or a whole hillside of terraces may cascade downwards.

Rice farming in each of these three main landscape types (mountain, valley plain, and hill terrace) is described in Chapters 3–5, together with some of the customs that surround it. Whether a farmer decides to broadcast seed or transplant, whether or not he practises crop rotation, and whether he harvests a crop once or twice a year depends not only on the

1. Transporting rice from forest field to longhouse, Sarawak. (Robert Schwenk, reproduced with the permission of V. Sutlive, from *The Iban of Sarawak*)

3

physical landscape, but also on that farmer's social and economic realities. How much land is farmed and how the work is done depends on how many people are available to work the land, and what their material needs are. There is no natural progression from, say, dibbling seeds in holes to broadcasting to transplanting—farmers simply adjust to current circumstances and then adjust again when the situation changes. Farmers in Malaysia and Central Thailand, for example, are now reverting to broadcasting seed rather than transplanting, because of shortages of labour power and the higher wages they must pay labourers.

Rice: The Staple Food

A rice grain consists of 82 per cent carbohydrate and about 10 per cent water. Then there is around 7 per cent protein and very small amounts of fibre, fat, and minerals. Compared with wheat and maize, rice is rather low in protein but otherwise the food value of the three cereal crops is similar. If rice appears to be less nutritious than other cereals, this is largely because much of the fat and protein is lost through milling, which is carried out to give a pure white product. The husk (also known as bran) is stripped away together with its useful oil. The aleurone layer or cuticle around the grain is similarly removed with the embryo. Additives such as talc or glucose may be used in the final 'polishing' process to get rid of the last of the rice bran. This polishing powder is removed when rice is washed before cooking.

The pounding that rice is subjected to in its preparation is likened to the effect of adversity on the human soul in this poem by a Vietnamese poet-politician:

How it suffers, the rice under the pounding of the pestle
But once this is over, how white it will be
So it is for a man, living in this world
To be a man, one must be pounded by misfortune.

(Ho Chi Minh, 1890 –1969)

It is well known that where rice is pounded by hand it is more nutritious, as less of the protein- and vitamin-rich cuticle that sur-

4

rounds the kernel of starch is lost (see Colour Plate 1). The people of Minangkabau (Sumatra) attribute the better taste of hand-pounded rice to the fact that the grains are so badly bruised and battered in a rice mill that the rice soul flees from the rice.

Rice steamers are traditionally made from bamboo but electric-powered metal steamers are now very common. Steaming is the preferred means of cooking rice as it retains what is left of the vitamins and protein after milling and polishing. Steaming cooks the grain at a slightly higher temperature than that of boiling water, so

2. Siamese ladies at dinner—dining in the traditional style, still used today. (From H. Mouhot, *Travels in the Central Parts of Indo-China, Cambodia and Laos*, London, John Murray, 1864; reprinted Singapore, Oxford University Press, 1989)

it is a faster process. Once steamed, rice may be eaten plain or mixed with tasty titbits and fried. In Malaysia and elsewhere, glutinous rice is cooked with meat in a bamboo joint over a fire. A Cambodian version of this (*kralan*) adds grated coconut and a few beans to the rice before cooking. Rice vermicelli is a staple of Chinese and South-East Asian cookery. *Mi fen* in Chinese, *sen mee* in Thai, these fine noodles are made from rice flour and are prepared by soaking in hot water for 10 minutes. The vermicelli may be eaten without further cooking, or it may be boiled briefly or deep-fried. There are various South-East Asian soups which add rice vermicelli to meat or fish bouillon and soy sauce, mixed herbs, and spices.

Rice is also served as rice flakes made from grilled, just-ripe rice pounded into flakes; crackly sheets of rice are produced in a similar way. A thin rice paste is used for feeding young children and babies from a very early age. Then there is rice for long journeys, which

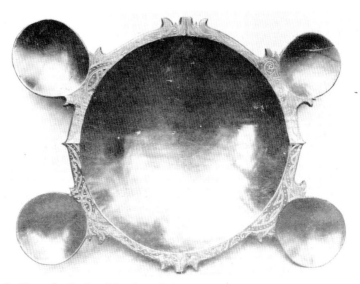

3. Kayan family rice dish of wood. (From C. Hose and W. McDougall, *The Pagan Tribes of Borneo*, London, Macmillan & Co., 1912; reprinted Singapore, Oxford University Press, 1993)

must keep fresh for several days. To achieve this, rice is cooked and then dried in the sun. Traditionally, it was packed into a bamboo joint for transport. Plate 2 shows a traditional-style dinner in Thailand in the late nineteenth century, but much the same scene could be found today. The Siamese ladies are dining off china plates. In Borneo, in approximately the same period, a wooden dish might have been used to hold rice and its accompaniments (see Plate 3).

A family of six could be fed from the yield of a farm of about 1 hectare provided it produces the average yield achieved in South-East Asia—about 1.5 tonnes per hectare using local varieties. Family rice farms are very small. Typically, a family's small plots will occupy between 0.4 and 2.4 hectares.

Other Uses of Rice

Rice is not only used for food. Alcohol is derived from rice (wine, beer, and spirits) and rice is needed for ceremonials. Some rice must, of course, be kept for sowing next year's crop; then any remainder may be sold to buy goods which cannot be obtained from the land.

Alcohol made from rice is used to celebrate marriages and annual rituals. Various types of rice wine are made across the region by steeping boiled glutinous rice in water, together with herbs and a cake made from very old, dry, finely ground rice containing fungi, yeasts, and spices. The mixture is left in open tubs whilst the desired alcoholic strength is reached (about a month); then it is decanted out into vessels which are closed and stored for several months. During the first phase, the fungi from the cake turn the grain starch into glucose in an aerobic process; in the second (anaerobic) phase in sealed containers, this glucose is converted into alcohol. In Cambodia, a variety of 'black' sticky rice is said to give the most delicately scented rice wine. Steady fermentation of sticky rice may achieve an alcohol content of around 20 per cent.

Rice wine may be distilled to give spirits such as arrack. In Central Borneo the Kelabit people distil strong drink from rice wine by using a series of cooking pots, bamboo tubes, and cold water. The resulting liquor is seen as something of a curiosity, rather than a drink to be taken widely. Distillation is used to give sake in Japan and *wang tsiu* in China. A form of rice beer is also made. The rice is boiled, spread out, and inoculated with 'cakes' of rice, fungi, and yeasts; then it is wrapped in leaves and kept moist. A sweet–sour liquid eventually drains out of the packets—it does not keep and is soon drunk.

The whiteness of rice makes it suitable for use as a cosmetic. Rice paste is often spread on the faces of adults and children during festivals, either to enhance the appearance or to provide protection from the heat. *Bedak sejuk* is a face powder traditionally made and used by Straits Chinese in Malaysia. Rice is soaked in water for some time and then finely ground into flour. The wet paste is packed into a device like a forcing bag for cake icing and squeezed out in the form of little round tablets, which are then set to dry on bamboo trays. The *bedak sejuk*, which may be perfumed, is eventually soaked in water to form a creamy paste for use.

Rice bran oil is a pale, colourless oil which may be used for cooking or making soap, though it can easily become rancid. The oil is also used as a vehicle for insecticides. Locally, husks may be used as a fuel for rice mills. New research in Thailand is looking at gasification of rice husks to produce energy.

Rice straw is used as an inferior livestock feed which may be improved by the addition of rice meal—the cuticle of the grain—plus the embryo, which are both removed from the grain during polishing. Rice straw is also used as a medium for growing 'straw mushrooms' in Thailand and China, as well as for bedding and litter for livestock. Rice-paper for documents, however, has nothing to do with rice: it is made from the pith of the rice-paper tree (*Tetrapanax papyrifera*) which is native to Taiwan and China. Edible rice-paper is made from rice flour and other starches.

The Rice Plant

Rice belongs to the family of grasses (Gramineae), as do the other major crops which have become staples of agricultural production (wheat, maize, barley, etc.). The rice plant forms a small clump, with several side-shoots or tillers developing from the base. The stems of the plant are usually between 50 and 150 centimetres tall, depending on the variety. Each stem has a flower spike made up of about 100 pale green spikelets, each of which should give a grain of rice after pollination. As rice flowers are usually self-pollinated or are pollinated by the wind, they do not have conspicuous colouring or scent to attract insects or birds. (This is also true of wheat and maize.) Self-pollination also means that the rice a farmer grows will breed true from year to year, as the offspring is produced from only one set of genes. Rice usually matures after about 4–5 months, but there are also varieties that ripen in as few as 3 months or as many as 7 months. In South-East Asia, rice is usually harvested by hand: this reduces the risk that the seed coats will open prematurely and shed their grain.

Subspecies

In the process of collecting seeds for sowing on prepared land, farmers in remote times learned to select those seed heads which did not ripen and shatter before harvest. Over millennia, selection for this and other characteristics such as taste, cooking qualities, size, and colour has meant that very many 'varieties' and races of rice have been built up. The Ayurvedic *Materia Medica*, written by Susrutha 3,000 years ago, distinguishes rice groups by duration of growing season, water requirements, and food values, showing that by 1000 BC there had already been considerable evolution and selection of cultivated varieties.

There are hundreds, maybe thousands, of different local varieties of rice; these can be grouped into three major subspecies: *indica*, *japonica*, and *javanica*. Each subspecies is suited to one of the major climatic types of South-East Asia and its varieties have particular growing and cooking characteristics which make them more or less valuable. The *indica* subspecies grow in tropical monsoon areas. Varieties of *indica* rice are very tolerant of difficult conditions, especially drought, and though yields are moderate, they command a high price—basmati rice comes in this group. *Indica* grains are long and slender and the rice plants tend to be tall and leafy with many side-shoots (or tillers) from the base. In choosing *indica* subspecies, the farmer is recognizing that although yields may be low, at least he can be sure of harvesting a crop.

The *javanica* subspecies are suited to equatorial areas where water is abundant throughout the year. They are very vulnerable to drought and give a stubbier rice grain. Yields of *javanica* are low and the crop commands only a medium price. Varieties of *japonica* rice, as the name suggests, are suited to growth in more temperate areas and this is the group taken to countries with dry summers and cool wet winters, such as Spain, Australia, and California. Typically, grains of *japonica* rice are broader and thicker than those of *indica* rice and whilst yields are high, their value is relatively low. The *japonica* rice plant is shorter, less likely to be blown down by the wind and rain, and it is less leafy than the *indica* rice plant.

Within individual subspecies groups, there are thousands of 'races' and varieties, each with a set of slightly different characteristics. These breed true from generation to generation and are valued because they fit the needs of a particular location—for example, some are tolerant of poor soils, while others can ripen during a short growing season. Scented rice is prized for special occasions and coloured grains may also be used for particular purposes (see Colour Plate 2).

The great diversity of traditional rice varieties gives security to the farmer: traditional varieties are better adapted to local climatic and soil conditions and to the diseases and pests found locally. In the early years of modern rice breeding, high production was the major aim. These hybrids can outperform the traditional varieties but they need water, fertilizers, and pesticides in abundance. Where small farmers cannot afford these inputs, they may well be better off with traditional varieties. More recent breeding work has concentrated on previously neglected characteristics like resistance to drought and disease.

The cooking qualities of the three main types of rice vary. Basmati is characteristic of *indica* rice and has long, narrow, and flattened grains of a translucent whiteness. Varieties of *indica* rice tend to cook without becoming too soft, which makes them attractive to importing countries. These hard, starchy grains make

4. Thai basket for sticky rice. (Denis Robinson)

up the bulk of traded rice. Some other rice varieties are more likely to become sticky in cooking and their colour is a chalky, opaque white. Within this group comes the so-called 'glutinous' or sticky rice—a misleading name as no gluten is present. However, this rice is very adherent, even jelly-like, when cooked. Plate 4 shows a Thai basket for carrying sticky rice. It is often the 'sticky' rice that has local importance for beer-making and ceremonial uses.

2
Rice in History and Culture

The Introduction of Rice Farming

BEFORE rice began its spread across South-East Asia, many of the early people living there relied on hunting and gathering in the forests. Gradually, farming was introduced as small-grain millets and tubers began to be cultivated rather than merely collected from the wild.

Archaeologists have been able to date the time when cereals were taken into cultivation and where these momentous events took place. The clues they use are grain prints on clay and mummified or carbonized remains, as well as the present-day distribution of the wild forms from which the cultivated crop has been developed. Crop archaeologists can tell us, for example, that wild forms of wheat began to be cultivated by Neolithic farmers 10,000 years ago in the Middle East, in lands between what are now Turkey and Israel. This is also the region in which wild forms of wheat such as einkorn are still most common.

The picture is less clear for rice. The early traces of rice that have been found suggest an origin somewhere in South or South-East Asia along a belt from Upper Assam in India, through Burma (Myanmar) and Thailand, into South-west China and North Vietnam. The wild species of rice are widely distributed over the warm and wet parts of India, South-East Asia, Indonesia, and southern China. Ancient rice grains have been located in the lower and central Yangtze Valley and radio-carbon dated to around 4000 BC. Abundant rice remains at the site of a Chinese village in the Yangtze Delta indicate that rice farming was already well established there in about 5000 BC. (Much later, in 148 BC, Ssu-ma Ch'ien described farming in the Yangtze Valley, 'where the land is tilled with fire and hoed with water'.) In North-east Thailand, rice imprints have been found at Nom Nok Tha and Ban Chiang and indicate that rice farming was well underway in the north-eastern plateau even before 4500 BC. At the western edges of its range in India and Pakistan, cultivated rice has been traced back to 2500–2000 BC. Thus it looks as though rice followed wheat into cultivation, though this may be the result of the lesser likelihood of grains being preserved in the wet tropical regions. The evidence suggests that rice farming started in marshy areas and then spread towards drier land and the hills as the farmers' expertise increased.

The advent of rice and the subsequent development of ways for controlling water on the land brought immense change. Great quantities of food could be grown, provided that people became settled farmers and invested much labour in the land. Instead of taking what could be found, they needed to prepare land and sow seeds they had collected the previous season. Eventually terracing had to be learned, as well as ploughing, transplanting, weeding, and means of keeping pests away.

Oxen and water-buffaloes were domesticated and trained to plough. Away from the marshes, the depredations of pests from the forest (birds, wild pigs, rats, and mice) became more damaging and tools and practices had to be developed to cope with this threat. Nevertheless, because of high yields and growing populations, rice farming spread up into the hills where terraces might be built. Then, it spread further into mountain forests where rice could still produce an acceptable crop with rainfall alone.

The Spread of Rice across Asia and the World

Descended from wild rice (perhaps *Oryza perennis*), cultivated rice spread gradually across the world—first, perhaps, into southern China, which had previously relied on millet. In classical Chinese, the terms 'agriculture' and 'rice cultivation' are synonymous, suggesting rice farming was already an important staple as the language developed. From China, rice spread towards the Philippines—the hill terraces of Luzon are believed to have been built by southern Chinese who migrated there in the second millennium BC. Rice did not reach Japan till relatively late—around 300–400 BC. Japan then became known as Mizumono Kuni—the Land of Luxurious Rice Crops. Rice became very important: '... next to the

Emperor, rice is the most sacred of all things on earth. Money can be squandered and the wastrel forgiven, but there is no forgiveness for wasting rice.'

Within South-East Asia, rice farming spread rather slowly southwards and tuber crops and millets remained the staple crops for a very long time. The ninth-century temple carvings at Borobudur, for example, show millet, rather than rice, being cultivated. It is believed that rice reached Java not from the north, but from India in the west during the later period of Hindu influence. Irrigated rice seems to have become established in Java shortly before the ascendancy of the Majapahit kingdom in the thirteenth century.

Beyond South-East Asia, there are ancient references to rice in Babylonia, Bactriana, and Lower Syria after 285 BC. A Chinese traveller, Can Kien, mentions rice in the southern parts of Central Asia at about the same time. The crop was known to the ancient Romans as a result of their conquests in the east and by the first century BC rice was being imported to Egypt from India. Subsequently, it was brought in by the Arabs and grown in the Nile Delta. Rice was taken to the coast of North Africa and northwards into Spain by the invading Moors as they spread westwards in the early Middle Ages. Rice may have been grown in Sicily since ancient times but it did not reach northern Italy till the fifteenth century, introduced either by Venetian traders or by Spaniards. Rice finally reached Australia and California in the early part of this century.

Production and Trade

In South-East Asia, rice is grown mainly by peasant farmers who keep most of it for their own families' subsistence and sell any remainder to pay for life's other necessities. Only about 5 per cent of the rice produced in the world is traded on international markets. Much of traded rice now comes from highly intensive agriculture; most of it is grown in the United States and Europe as well as India, though peasant-based production in Thailand still constitutes a major source for world markets. Some of the rice economies of South and South-East Asia no longer produce sufficient rice for their own needs. Others, like India, produce and export high-quality rice but also import lower-quality rice for domestic consumption. Malaysia and Sri Lanka now have to import. Burma, once an important exporter, has seen its surplus cut by the national decline of agriculture. Indonesia's surplus has vanished as its population has increased. Cambodia exported rice steadily before the 1970s, but its potential has been severely diminished by years of neglect and the aftermath of war. China's peasants produce most of the world's rice crop (about 56 million tonnes) but China only imports or exports in exceptional years.

Although most of the rice of South-East Asia is consumed at home and never reaches the market, rice has been important in shaping export trading links between countries and the development of land.

The state of Siam was already exporting rice to Malacca and other ports in the sixteenth century. Until the mid-nineteenth century, this and other types of international trade were controlled by the kings. During the Ayutthaya period (AD 1350–1767), canals were built from the royal seat at Ayutthaya to the coast, through the largely uninhabited Chao Phraya Delta, in order to speed transport to the Gulf of Thailand. The Bowring Treaty of 1855 ended the royal trade monopoly and so contributed to an expansion of rice-growing schemes across the delta. Canals and drainage schemes ceased to be funded exclusively by the monarchy but were built by entrepreneurs—Siamese nobles and Chinese merchants—who received concessions from the king. In the late nineteenth century, settlement of the delta progressed as more canals made irrigation and rice cultivation possible.

In a similar way, the rulers of Kedah, Malaysia, built canals across the Muda Plain from the seventeenth century in order to promote rice cultivation. Kedah rice was then exported via the East India Company in Penang. This scheme has been expanded in the latter half of the twentieth century, as the demand for rice continues to grow.

Rice and Social Change

The move from gathering food to farming the land was accompanied by great changes in social structures and patterns. When populations settled, they could acquire more belongings but they became tied to the land in which they had invested time for weeding and planting. Populations grew more rapidly than among nomadic hunter-gatherers; in particular, women could have babies more frequently when the need to carry infants long distances was reduced. Nevertheless, disease became a greater problem and some evidence provided by human skeletons from this distant past suggests that the hunter-gatherer's diet produced healthier, larger individuals, though there were fewer of them.

Settled agriculture producing surplus food eventually led to the development of civilizations, societies, and hierarchies of protectors and protected: kings, priests, and soldiers, all fed by farmers. Where yields were good, some people could be spared from the rice-fields for the manufacture of arts and handicrafts. As societies developed, with élite groups of royalty, administrators, and religious persons, the arts flourished and eventually attracted contact with a wider world.

The Beginnings of Irrigation

It is not difficult to imagine river flood waters being used from early times to provide natural irrigation for rice. From there it seems a small step to the building of bunds and dams to retain water longer in fields. Then, to get round the problem of seasonal rainfall, tanks and reservoirs would be built to save water to irrigate fields in times of shortage.

As ways of controlling water were developed, societies changed further, investing ever more in the land for terracing, transplanting rice, and eradicating pests. Erratic harvests were replaced by more reliable harvests; greater numbers of people could be supported by the land and, hand in hand with this, more people were needed to provide the labour to work the irrigation systems.

The great kingdoms of South-East Asia have usually been based on irrigated rice production. In Burma in the sixth century, an irrigation system was set up at Pyu. Similarly Pagan, the major religious site of more than five thousand temples on a bend in the Irrawaddy River, dominated western Burma from the ninth to the thirteenth century. Pagan's hegemony was also based on an irrigation system which increased rice yields over a very large area and so supported a hierarchy of priests and princes and a burgeoning population. At about the same time as Pagan was powerful in the west of the region, another great complex was being created in the east: Angkor, built when the Khmers were expanding their power. The city of Angkor was sited on the fertile plain to the north of the Great Lake of Cambodia, which was renowned for its fisheries. Water for irrigation came from several rivers. The city and irrigation works were built by King Indravarman, who reigned from AD 877 to AD 889. It is the responsibility of a Hindu king to increase the wealth and contentment of his subjects, and so follow the example of Rama. This has been achieved principally by developing farming land. At Angkor a series of *baray* (artificial reservoirs) were built, their shape determined by Hindu cosmology. In the centre of each was a 'temple mountain' (*mebon*). From the *baray*, the waters were distributed in canals south-eastward across the plain.

Where tanks and canals are allowed to silt up, the life of an irrigation scheme is limited. It is believed that silt contributed to the eventual downfall of Angkor to the invading Siamese in AD 1364. Where canals are dredged and maintained, a scheme can endure for centuries. Perhaps the oldest is in China. The irrigation scheme at Guanxian (Sichuan), on a tributary of the Yangtze River, was started in 250 BC and finished 10 years later. It is still in use today and the prescriptions laid down by its founder for annual maintenance work to de-silt the canals are still followed closely.

Ceremonies

Not only does a good harvest of rice mean that the people will have enough to eat in the coming year, it also means that they will be able to organize and celebrate major rituals, as these always require copious amounts of rice.

The role of rice as the underpinning of social structures in South-East Asia is acknowledged in a hundred ways by the people who live there. Even in the centre of the modern metropolis that is Bangkok, the annual Royal Ploughing Ceremony brings the Thai King to attend a rice-planting ceremony using a team of gorgeously attired oxen and men (see Chapter 4). At his marriage in 1990, a Japanese prince carried a rice scoop to symbolize fertility. Rice, rather than wheat, is sometimes thrown at weddings in the West. Rice is incorporated as a symbol into designs and artefacts,

5. Malaysian textile design—the rhomboid motifs depict rice cakes made from glutinous rice. (From G. Selvanayagam, *Songket: Malaysia's Woven Treasure*, Singapore, Oxford University Press, 1990)

and the activities of cultivation are often brought into dance and the rituals of common life.

A ceremonial food, rice cakes are popular as symbols of long life, happiness, and abundance, despite being very bland. Being associated with these good things, rice cakes are then taken up in art: a rhomboid-shaped design is very common in woven Malaysian textiles, decorating the side panels. This rhomboid shape is taken from the small cakes of glutinous rice which are made in shallow trays or in cylinders of bamboo, then sliced and proffered on special occasions (see Plate 5).

Arts and Crafts

Rice and its production is a powerful symbol for the South-East Asian farmers who spend much of their lives tending the plant and who rely on rice for their staple food.

The equipment and articles involved in rice production and consumption are all important items in a South-East Asian household: the plough and harrow, baskets for winnowing or storing the seed, the pounding block, the rice bowl, and the steamer. Some of these items are used in decorating household goods such as baskets or textiles. Figure 1 reproduces some Iban designs associated with rice and used in textiles.

Plate 6 shows a woven blanket or *pua* from Sarawak. Used in ceremonies, *pua* also serve as screens to mark off an area of the Iban longhouse reserved for special occasions. This blanket, known as 'Bali-Belumpong', has two blocks of textile woven in colours, a plain central block, and long borders which depict leaves of rattan. The motif in the two-patterned blocks is the *entilang plangka*, the wooden mortar used for husking rice (see also Figure 1). The upper patterned block is topped with piles of pounded rice; the bottom row of the lower patterned block is intended to represent rice plants. Another *pua* is shown in Colour Plate 3; here the main motif is the *engkaramba* or spirit figure. The bottom row of motifs comprises rows of rice planting sticks, alternating with stalks or grains of rice. Small white particles may be woven into *pua* motifs and are referred to as rice grains.

6. Iban *pua* textile. The design in the two sections depicts the *entilang plangka* or mortar for husking rice. The top motif shows mounds of piled rice. (Reproduced with the permission of the Sarawak Museum, Kuching)

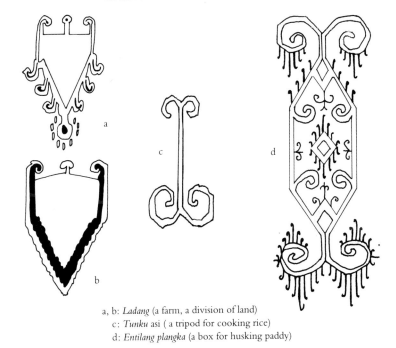

a, b: *Ladang* (a farm, a division of land)
   c: *Tunku* asi (a tripod for cooking rice)
   d: *Entilang plangka* (a box for husking paddy)

Fig. 1 Some motifs used in Iban basketry. (From A. C. Haddon and
   L. E. Start, *Iban or Sea Dayak Fabrics and Their Patterns*, Cambridge,
   Cambridge University Press, 1936)

Plate 7 shows a Malaysian sarong on which the central panel or
kepala is decorated with sheaves of rice. Also in the field of textiles,
rice paste is used in the Sunda Islands in the manufacture of fabrics
for *kain simbut* batik.

Basket weaving is another craft that borrows from rice farming.
Colour Plate 4 shows Laotian baskets while Colour Plate 5
shows two Kelabit baskets—one decorated, the other plain. Two
motifs taken from the rice-field and used in basket weaving are the
hoe and the leech. Iban baskets for carrying seed to the rice-field
are shown in Plate 8.

In a region where large green leaves still often serve in prefer-
ence to china, rice bowls and dishes are crafted with care to make

7. Malaysian sarong, *kepala* (central panel) design showing stalks of rice. (From G. Selvanayagam, *Songket: Malaysia's Woven Treasure*, Singapore, Oxford University Press, 1990)

vessels that are as light and agreeable as possible to handle, in addition to being beautifully glazed. There is a bowl design which incorporates the idea of the translucency of cooked rice. This popular bowl is made by incising patterns of grain-shaped holes in the clay before it dries. After the first firing, the small holes are skilfully glazed over, leaving patterns of translucent spots. The Bencharong rice bowl shown in Colour Plate 6 is a far more exclusive item, dating from the eighteenth to the nineteenth century. Plates 9 and 10 and Colour Plate 7 illustrate the range of materials used for making rice servers across the region—from coconut shell to silver.

Finally, contemporary South-East Asian painters frequently turn to the countryside, to rice farming and its traditions, for their inspiration. Colour Plate 8, painted by an Indonesian artist, shows Balinese rice-fields or *sawah*.

8. Baskets made by the Iban. The one on the left is a seed basket (*raga*) finely plaited and decorated with symbols which depict rice farming. (Reproduced with the permission of the Sarawak Museum, Kuching)

9. Silver and horn rice server, Kelantan, Malaysia. (Denis Robinson)

10. Rice server from Java, with wooden handle and coconut shell bowl. (Denis Robinson)

From this rapid survey of social customs, as well as arts and crafts, we see how deeply rice penetrates into South-East Asian cultures and feeds not only bodies but imaginations.

3
Farms in the Forest

Shifting Cultivation

IN some parts of South-East Asia, there are still hill farmers whose rice, watered only by rain, is grown on small plots within forests where the trees have just been cleared. This is known as shifting agriculture or slash-and-burn agriculture. Forest is felled and burned and the ash fertilizes the soil. Rice and vegetables are grown for a few years before the farmer's family moves on to another plot, leaving the forest to grow back as best it can over 15–20 years. It is then fired again. Slash-and-burn farmers are everywhere under pressure from governments to cease the practice and to settle on land and farm it intensively. Many believe that slash-and-burn farming wastes land and damages the environment as steep slopes are left bare, exposed to heavy rains and the risk of erosion. Rice farming in the uplands produces only about 5 per cent of the world's rice crop but covers some 8 million hectares in South-East Asia.

It is the very success of shifting cultivation that has made it a hazard. Yields from the burned-over land can be very good, so there is no incentive to change the methods used until there is no more 'new' land left—when there is no more virgin forest to fell. Social customs encourage farmers with good harvests to share them with the less successful farmers. Within a community, there will usually be enough food to ensure that the population can multiply. With this increase comes greater pressure on the land: the resting period may need to be shortened as families grow or as people from other families encroach. When the forest does not have enough time to regenerate, then rice yields decline and instead of taking a crop from a plot for 2 or 3 years, families have to move on faster. This means they complete their cycle through a series of plots more rapidly and return to the first plot sooner than would be advisable. This sets up a vicious circle which can only be avoided

25

whilst populations are small and there is land to spare.

Whilst shifting agriculture may sound rather simple, it does in fact involve a deep knowledge of the varieties of rice produced and complex procedures for harvesting the crop. Slash-and-burn farming is closely tied up with spiritual beliefs, ceremonies, and social behaviour which enable the land to be equitably shared out and neighbours' rights to be respected.

Customary Beliefs

It is thought-provoking to remember that much of Asia and Europe too were once farmed by slash-and-burn methods and there may well be concurrences between the beliefs of these distant farmers and the other South-East Asians who practise slash-and-burn today. For example, almost all cereal-growing societies believe in the existence of a female goddess, the 'mother of the grain'. This is Ceres in the Graeco-Roman tradition and the Corn Mother of the Anglo-Saxons (wheat), Dewi Sri in Thailand and Bok Sri in Java (rice), and the Corn Maiden of various American Indian peoples (maize).

The beliefs and rituals of slash-and-burn farmers in South-East Asia are particularly rich. Even parts of South-East Asia distant from each other, such as Sarawak and Cambodia, share some elements of the hill farmers' beliefs. Most important, perhaps, is the widespread belief in the rice soul, a living principle which makes the rice grow.

Legends of the origins of rice and how it came to be cultivated are recounted in myths by all the peoples of South-East Asia. Here is one such story from the Sentah people of Sarawak, abbreviated from an account collected by Henry Ling Roth at the end of the nineteenth century:

Once upon a time, Dayak mankind ate nothing but a fungus which grows on tree-trunks, together with roots, fruits and pith they collected and animals they snared. One day a number of men went sailing out to sea, among them young Se Juru. They were driven by the wind far out to sea till they came to a place where they heard the roar of a whirlpool and they saw a large *sibau* tree loaded with fruit, its roots in the sky and its branches touching the water.

Urged by his companions, Se Juru got up among the branches to gather some fruit; he continued there a long time, climbing higher and higher despite the remonstrances of his companions. At last they got tired of waiting and away they went without him. Here was a fix!

Se Juru, however, climbed on undeterred, determined to see what was at the end of the trunk and what it was rooted upon. At length he came to a new and beautiful place in the sky: the land of the Pleiades, the Seven Stars. While gazing about him in wonder and admiration, he was accosted by Se Kera, who took him to his house—which was built Dayak fashion—and set a cooking pot on the fire. After a time the contents of the pot were turned into a dish, and a mass of soft white grains appeared, heaped up together.

'Eat,' said Se Kera.

'Eat what?' asked Se Juru.

'That in the dish,' said Se Kera.

'What, those maggots?'

'Don't be a fool—that's not maggots, it's boiled rice.'

Se Kera explained to Se Juru how to plant and reap rice, how to pound it, and then cook it for food. Just then, Se Kera's wife went out to get some water and Se Juru looked into a large jar standing near him. To his wonder he could see, as through a telescope, his family assembled together and talking. Se Juru became homesick and lost his appetite for the rice until he was told all would be well. He thereupon made a hearty meal and prepared to return home. First Se Kera instructed him in all the mysteries of farming, taught him the use of bird-omens, told him how to cut down and burn the forest, how to reap and store the rice. After giving Se Juru three different kinds of rice, Se Kera let Se Juru down to earth by a long rope and he landed safe, close to his own village of Simpok. Since that time the Dayaks farm according to the instructions of Se Kera.

The ceremonies and beliefs of several groups of slash-and-burn farmers have been carefully observed. The Iban, who make up approximately one-third of the population of Sarawak, traditionally use shifting cultivation, and many of their practices and customs still continue today, though threatened by the logging of Sarawak's rain forest.

The Iban choose to live in longhouses in the river valleys, surrounded by dense forest on steeply sloping hills. A longhouse is not the home of a large extended family, but rather a 'street' or terrace of individual homes, each occupied by a small family; neighbours are not always relatives.

Each year, new land for burning is parcelled out by general agreement within the longhouse—Iban society is democratic, without a hierarchy of leadership. Each household lays claim to an area (perhaps a hillside from river to ridge), then commences clearing it. In the first year, land of perhaps 1.5–2.0 hectares is cleared. In the second year, some of the first-year land is reused and some more land cleared, perhaps only 1 hectare. Once a family has cleared virgin forest, it retains a right to return to it in the future. As the hillside is cleared, the family may open up new areas elsewhere for additional land. If the new plots are too far from the longhouse for regular daily journeys, a subsidiary longhouse may be built.

The Iban carry out their planting according to the movement of the constellations. According to an Iban man, speaking in 1949, 'If there were no stars, we Iban would be lost, not knowing when to plant; we live by the stars.'

The main dates of the farming calendar are felling, firing, planting, and harvesting. Felling commences in early June, and traditionally the time to fell is determined by the first appearance of the Pleiades over the horizon. First, the thin-stemmed undergrowth is cut with a knife; then successively larger trees are cut till only the biggest trees remain. Felling the forest giants is seen as a manly activity (as head-hunting once was) which requires skill and courage.

The felled forest and brush is left to dry out, though drying may be incomplete in the rain forest environment, with 150 inches (3 500 millimetres) of rain falling each year and only a slightly drier period in June and July. The community judges when the timber and branches are as dry as can be hoped, and then firing begins. A good burn is the secret of a good harvest. If the wood and undergrowth burn incompletely, then less ash is available to fertilize the soil. A poor burn also means harder work for the women who plant the seeds, as they have to scramble over large, half-burned logs. Plate 11 shows a cleared plot, soon after planting.

11. Shifting cultivators' plot after rice planting—planting and harvesting are not easy on such terrain. (Reproduced with the permission of the International Rice Research Institute, Manila)

When the Pleiades reach the zenith, dibbling (making seed holes) should commence and should be completed before Orion reaches the zenith. This means that dibbling and sowing seed should take place during September. In fact this date may be over-stepped if burning has not been successful, though the Iban say that rice will not ripen properly if planted after Sirius has reached the zenith in mid-October.

Felling, firing, and dibbling are seen as jobs for men. The man of the household strides across the field with a dibble stick—this is a hardwood staff about 1.5 metres long and sharpened to a point (see Plate 12). With a thrust and a flick of the wrist, a planting hole is made. A series of holes are made on either side at a rate of up to 60 holes a minute. Behind the dibbler follow the women of the household (normally the wife and her mother or eldest daughter) carrying baskets of rice seeds. They must bend low to flick a few seeds into each hole and achieve an even distribution of rice across

12. Iban man making planting holes for rice with dibbling stick. (Robert Schwenk, reproduced with the permission of V. Sutlive, from *The Iban of Sarawak*)

the field. Mixed in with the rice seeds may be seeds of cucumber, pumpkin, and other gourds.

Several distinct rice varieties may be planted by a family, for they are to fulfil different needs. The rice seeds the women sow have been saved in the family's granary from the previous year. Seeds of each variety used are kept in separate containers. Planted first are a few sections of glutinous rice, as the Iban know they grow best in the early part of the season. Next, the fast-growing varieties are planted to provide the first of the new season's crops 4 or 5 months later. These are in turn followed by a larger area made up of a number of 'ordinary' rice varieties which will provide the bulk of the family's diet over the coming year. The timing and location of this sowing must be carefully planned so that different areas will ripen at different times, spreading the work of harvesting over a period of months, from mid-February to mid-April.

Finally, the two types of ritual rice are sown in a small area. Each family has its own 'sacred rice' (*padi pun*), which may be distinguished by its colour or other characteristics, such as the number of heads of rice or the length of stem. Sowing the sacred rice is perhaps the most important rite of the Iban family's year. The sacred rice may have its own myth which may suggest some supernatural origin. It is protected by a series of prohibitions and acts of respect and deference. For example, sacred rice is not handled by men, it is never sold, and some is retained from a year's sowing, to ensure that there will be some for the following year even if the *padi pun* crop should fail. The location of the *padi pun* becomes the sacred heart of the farm; it is surrounded by rice used for secondary ceremonials called *padi sangking*. Around this sacred centre are planted 'magical plants' which also have ceremonial and ritual significance and which guard and succour the growing rice.

This planting pattern already looks much more complex than that of the modern cereal farmers sowing a single variety of wheat across broad acres. But a further complication is added: for the Iban, the pattern of ripening and harvest must be such that the reapers will meet with no break in their path. They must progress across or around the farm along a single line, moving from section to section as each ripens, then finally reaching the sacred rice at the end of the harvest period. The reason for this is that the Iban believe that the souls of the rice a woman has harvested must follow her and not be permitted to stray or next year's crop will be the poorer. An unbroken route is followed and where an uncultivated stretch, such as a path, crosses a field, the spirits must be provided with a bridge across the bare land—in this case, a bamboo pole is placed from crop to crop and the spirits are encouraged along it by singing, prayers, and offerings. The rice is cut by hand with a small knife half hidden in the palm so as not to frighten or offend the rice soul (see Plate 13).

At last, after harvesting has progressed around the fields over several weeks, only the *padi pun* remains; it is believed that by now the spirits of all the harvested rice will have congregated in this

13. Harvesting rice with a concealed knife, Sarawak. (Robert Schwenk, reproduced with the permission of V. Sutlive, from *The Iban of Sarawak*)

32

area. The sacred rice is then duly reaped and the rice spirits are con-
ducted back to the granary with appropriate ceremony.

The senior woman of the family is responsible for devising the
planting pattern as well as for storing the harvested rice. She will
have great knowledge of local rice varieties. Men are usually not
allowed into the granary and until they reach middle age may
know relatively little about rice farming. Young men may refuse to
participate in tasks like weeding which are seen as 'women's
work'. Young men see the period between planting and harvesting
as a time for travelling. The men leave to work on rubber planta-
tions or go abroad, so that they can gain prestige and earn the
money to buy status symbols—traditionally, these included
Chinese jars and brass gongs.

Men will generally return to the farm for the harvest—to help
transport the heavy baskets of rice back to the family home (see
Plate 1) and to assist in the threshing, winnowing, and pressing of
the rice into containers, and then the lifting of these to the loft

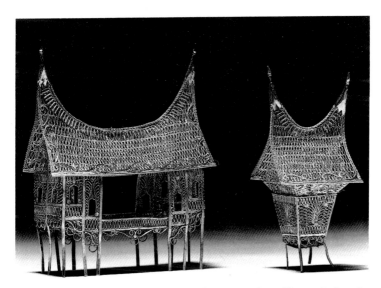

14. Rice granary and village meeting house in silver filigree, Indonesia.
(Reproduced with the permission of the Tropenmuseum, Amsterdam)

which acts as the granary. Granary design varies considerably across South-East Asia, depending on local materials and building practices. Colour Plate 9 shows a particularly splendid house with rice barns in the uplands of West Sumatra; compare this with the silver filigree barn shown in Plate 14 and the Balinese granary shown in Plate 23.

Other South-East Asian Shifting Cultivators

The above account describes a little of the rice-growing culture of the Iban shifting cultivator. Similar methods are used on hill land elsewhere in South-East Asia—wherever farmers are poor but have plenty of 'free' labour available, either within the family or within a close community, and wherever the land can provide a reasonable crop with only the ash of burned forest to fertilize the soil. For there to be forest to burn, of course, some land must be left fallow for many years, thereby allowing the forest to return. Farming methods vary slightly but the similarities are greater than the differences.

In the Philippines, for example, the Bagobos people plant their rice as a community after they have burned the trees. The planters advance in line across the field to the accompaniment of music. Holes are driven into the ground with bamboo sticks split at the top and the split ends clack together in time to the music. The seed is then dropped into the holes by women and covered with the foot. This is known as *caingin* farming and in the Philippines *caingin* rice is often grown in mixtures with crops such as Job's tears (another cereal) or with cotton or maize.

The Brou people of North-east Cambodia also practise shifting cultivation, but in a more gently rolling landscape than the Iban. Here, the land is covered with secondary forest, that is, forest that has already been cut over and fired for agriculture. For the Brou people, the spirit world is populated with *arak*, minor spirits attached to a particular location, who may be disturbed by farming operations. Then there are the *yaa*, the ancestors, who inhabit the celestial sphere.

When forest is to be cleared, it is marked—for example, by placing a branch across a notch in a tree. Once this has been done, a group can be confident it will be respected by neighbouring farmers seeking land to clear. The local *arak* are informed and propitiated with offerings. A number of ceremonial articles are piled together—a knife, the legs of a slaughtered chicken, an axe and a banana shoot, shavings of wood from adjacent trees. Chicken blood is poured over them and the farmer begins an incantation which is addressed to the ancestors and spirits of the locality:

Oh Spirits of this place
I am marking the forest
Wait for the tobacco to ripen
Wait for the rice to grow
May our dreams be favourable
We will cut the trees
May the rice be as abundant as grains of sand
    hard as sacred stones, hard as iron
I shall stay in this place: I am marking the forest
Let me stay here
May the ginger grow, may the garlic become fat
When we have sown tobacco, may we gather it
When we have planted rice, may we harvest it
I mark the forest, I am going to fell the trees,
Ancestors, Spirits of this place!

(Translated from J. Matras-Troubetzkoy, *Un village en forêt*, 1983)

Whether or not the spirits of a section of forest have given their consent will be indicated in dreams the following night. A dream involving a large animal, an elephant or a buffalo, for example, is likely to be considered a favourable dream, as is a dream of a large expanse of water.

As with the Iban, dibbling holes for rice seeds is a particularly male preserve and a household without men must call upon a brother or other relative to help. Here again the women progress across the field bent low, carrying their grains in one hand in a hollow bamboo tube closed at one end. They use this tube to cover

over the seeds as they pass. In the months after sowing, the principal occupations of the Brou are weeding, pest control, the cultivation of fruit and vegetable gardens, and the construction of new houses and fences around the village. Finally, harvest approaches and another period of rituals and ceremonies begins. As elsewhere in South-East Asia, the time when the first rice is harvested is a time for general festivity and marriages are celebrated. When a young man marries, he is presented with a pair of decorated dibble sticks by his father and these remain an important personal possession that he will use for several years.

A ceremonial offering is usually set up in the paddy-field as thanks for the harvest. This is often in the form of a bamboo pole with its upper section split in several places lengthwise and the slats bent outwards and fixed to make a funnel shape similar to a fish trap. The funnel is then filled with traditional offerings to the rice spirit: beer and chicken.

Before rice is stored, the straw and awns (stiff hairs) must be separated from the grain by threshing—this is traditionally done in the region by foot, usually by men. After it has been dried for several days in the sun, a small quantity of rice is poured into large flat sieves or riddles of basketwork and trodden beneath the feet for several minutes. The grain passes through the basketwork, while the straw is retained. Next, the sieved rice is winnowed to remove any empty husks. The Indo-Chinese girl in Plate 15 interrupted her winnowing to be photographed in the mid-1870s.

Finally, the rice is stored in circular bins of woven bamboo. Both Iban and Brou believe that the rice soul is capable of increasing or diminishing the quantity of rice stored in the granary and prayers will be offered for its increase. Take, for example, this delightfully insouciant Brou prayer:

Hail Yaa Jung Chroo
I am celebrating the raising of the rice to the granary
May it fill the farm house
May it overflow
May the beams break and the floor give way.
We will build another.

1. Kenyah women husking paddy. (From C. Hose and W. McDougall, *The Pagan Tribes of Borneo*, London, Macmillan & Co., 1912; reprinted Singapore, Oxford University Press, 1993)

2. Grains of rice of different varieties. There are many other colours and shapes than those shown here. (Reproduced with the permission of the International Rice Research Institute, Manila)

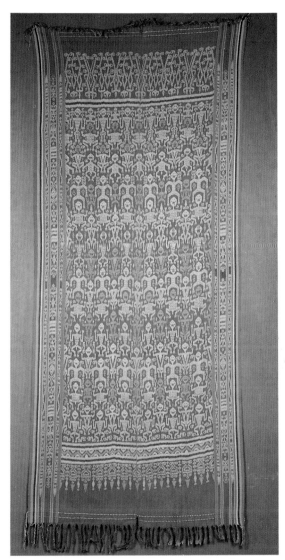

3. Iban *pua* textile. The bottom row of motifs consists of paddy-planting
   sticks with the sharp ends in blue, alternating with stalks or rice grains.
   (Reproduced with the permission of the Sarawak Museum, Kuching)

4. Baskets for sticky rice, Laos. (Denis Robinson)

5. Kelabit carrying baskets (Sarawak). The cone-shaped basket is decorated with symbols related to growing rice. (Reproduced with the permission of the Sarawak Museum, Kuching)

6. Bencharong porcelain rice bowl, white glazed interior with a small lotus motif in the centre. Eighteenth to nineteenth century, Thailand. Height 5.8 cm. (Denis Robinson)

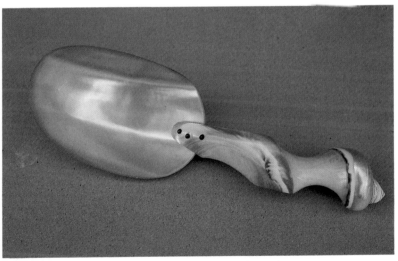

7. Rice server made from shell, Thailand. (Denis Robinson)

8. *Sawah* (rice-fields). Acrylic on canvas, 75 × 56 cm. Made Sinteg, Penestanan, 1985. (Reproduced with the permission of Dr A. A. M. Djelantik, Walter Spies Foundation)

9. House and rice barns, Minangkabau highlands, West Sumatra. (Roxanna Waterson)

10. Lifting water manually to the paddy-field, Vietnam. (Ric Vokes)

11. Transplanting rice, Vietnam. (Ric Vokes)

12. Royal Ploughing Ceremony, Bangkok, Thailand. (Courtesy of Chaiyuth Sukhsri)

13. Buffaloes ploughing a field to creamy mud. (Reproduced with the permission of the Royal Thai Embassy, London)

14. Treeless rice terraces in Luzon, Philippines. (Ric Vokes)

15. Rice terraces in Bali. (David Warrell)

16. Transplanting rice on a terrace in the Philippines. (Reproduced with the permission of the International Rice Research Institute, Manila)

17. A traditional bird-scaring device—children posted in the shelter pull on cords bedecked with scraps of cloth which stretch over the crop. (From M. T. H. Perelaer, *Het Kamerlid Van Berkenstein in Nederlansch-Indie*, Leiden, 1888–9)

18. Balinese *jaja*—ceremonial biscuits made from rice paste. (From F. Brinkgreve and D. J. Stuart-Fox, *Offerings: The Ritual Art of Bali*, Jakarta,
Image Network Indonesia, 1992)

20. *Pokok nasi*—ceremonial offering presented at a Malaysian wedding. (Reproduced with the permission of Ghulam-Sarwar Yousof)

19. Balinese offering, with multicoloured cones of cooked rice. (From F. Brinkgreve and D. J. Stuart-Fox, *Offerings: The Ritual Art of Bali*, Jakarta, Image Network Indonesia, 1992)

21. Wooden image of the Rice God from the Philippines. (Ric Vokes)

22. Field shrine to the Rice Goddess, Dewi Sri, Bali. (David Warrell)

23. Iban devil mask with inserted side panels, Sarawak, made of polychromed wood. Height 36 cm. Private collection, New York. (Reproduced with the permission of Irwin Hersey)

24. Dance after the rice harvest, Central Plains of Thailand. (Reproduced with the permission of the Royal Thai Embassy, London)

15. Indo-Chinese girl winnowing rice, photographed in the mid-1870s. (John Thomson)

To Yaa Jung Chroo is attributed the gift of rice to men; he showed them how to grow, harvest, and prepare it. Yaa Jung Chroo is the Lord of the Heavens who is believed to control the rain. A secondary figure is Yaa Cing Iar, an elderly widow who cares for an orphan, Mbee. Yaa Cing Iar is credited with giving women the art of weaving and knowledge of plants and insects. It is her face that is said to be visible on the full moon.

For the Rungao people in Vietnam, the shadows on the moon represent the goddess heaping up her rice in the shade of a Bo tree. In Rungao myth, a poverty-stricken widow welcomed the Lord of the Heavens, together with the God of Thunder, Krung Yung, to her miserable home. In recognition of this, the two gods taught her how to ensure a good harvest. They recommended that a cotton thread be stretched from field to granary: once this was done, it would be unnecessary for the rice to be carried to the granary, as each grain would follow the thread itself, as though carried by an invisible ant. Unfortunately, rice can no longer be expected to transport itself but the thread is still provided for the rice spirit to make the journey.

The God of Thunder, incidentally, is a redoubtable hunter and thunder in the hills is taken to be the sound of Krung Yung hunting on his elephant, using a small axe. Such axes, made of polished stone, are frequently found in northern Cambodia and are believed to date from prehistoric times.

Measuring Time

Whilst the Iban and Thai hill-tribe folk traditionally used the stars as a seasonal clock, the inhabitants of Central Borneo looked to the height of the sun in the daytime. Baluy-Kayan people set up a standing stone as a gnomon, and when its shadow reached either of two specific lengths, the time had come for planting. Other Kayan groups used two stones of unequal height and judged that planting time had arrived when the sun was aligned with the apex of both stones. Plate 16, photographed in Borneo at the beginning of this century, shows two men measuring the length of the sun's shadow

16. Using a gnomon to assess the height of the sun as an indicator of the time
to plant seed. (From C. Hose and W. McDougall, *The Pagan Tribes of
Borneo*, London, Macmillan & Co., 1912; reprinted Singapore, Oxford
University Press, 1993)

at noon in order to tell whether or not the time has come to commence sowing. The job of observing the changing seasons was considered so onerous that the 'weatherman' responsible for this task did not farm but was provided with rice by others. He used an *aso do*, a pole set and secured vertically in flat ground. The height of the pole equalled the distance from fingertip to fingertip across the weatherman's body. Every three days, the length of the midday sun was observed by using another stick, as long as the weatherman's arm. When the shadow of the *aso do* equalled half the length of the weatherman's arm, ploughing time had come.

Such an intricate system for measuring time, in a society that had not calculated the number of days in a year, must make us pause and wonder. Equally thought-provoking is a system used by the Klemantan people at about the same time. A bamboo pole was first filled to the top with water; then, with one end resting on the ground, it was pointed towards a particular star. Water would spill out. When the pole was returned to the upright position, the height of the water within the pole would be lower. Sowing time was deemed to have arrived once the water had fallen to a level marked previously on the pole and set over years of experience.

Another method used in Central Borneo was also based on the height of the midday sun. By regularly measuring the distance between the point where a beam of midday sunlight passing through a hole in the roof strikes the floor, and the point vertically below that hole, the progress of the year could be gauged. Once a specific distance had been achieved between the two points (in other words, when the midday sun was at a particular angle in the sky), then planting time had come.

Incidentally, to those who had no calendar, the passage of the years was marked and remembered by the rice harvests. In shifting cultivation, the family moves to some new land each year. In the early years of this century, one observer noted that the Kayan people of Borneo would calculate their children's ages by counting up the number of harvests on different patches of land since each child's birth.

4
Farming the Flood

The scholar precedes the peasant,
but when the rice runs out
it's the peasant who precedes the scholar.

(Vietnamese proverb)

Cultivating the Flood Plain

THE flood plains of the great rivers of South-East Asia are home to the world's highest densities of human populations. Though many of these people are housed within the teeming cities, even greater numbers live in rural areas and depend on rice farming for a living.

On the flood plains, the regular seasonal overflow of the rivers provides natural irrigation water, and farmers can sow a wide area with rice seed and hope to harvest it. The yield will not be as high as with the transplanted rice of intensively worked, artificially irrigated plots. However, because less effort needs to be put into each plot of land, a larger area can be sown, and so the total amount harvested can be high.

Rice is unique among man's food crops in that it can grow in water. The water prevents weed growth but would drown most crops. Algae in the flooded fields work to help the rice grow. Blue-green algae fertilize the rice by making nitrogen whilst green algae oxygenate the water. After harvest, weeds are allowed to grow on the land for a time before being ploughed in. The ploughed-in weeds decay under the soil and help fertilize the land for the next crop. Animal manure may also be added or ducks and fish kept. By these means, rice can be grown year after year on the same soil without depleting its fertility. This contrasts strongly with modern Western cereal farming, where expensive inputs must be added each year and the land gradually loses its fertility.

41

Long ago an anonymous Vietnamese peasant-poet, probably a woman, wrote this account of the farming year:

The twelfth moon for potato growing
   the first for beans, the second for eggplant
In the third we break the land
   to plant rice in the fourth while the rains are strong.
The man ploughs, the woman plants
   and in the fifth: the harvest and the gods are good
   an acre yields five full baskets this year.
I grind and pound the paddy, strew husks to cover the manure
   and feed the hogs with bran.
Next year, if the land bears extravagantly well
   I shall pay the taxes for you.
In plenty or in want, there will still be you and me
   always the two of us
Is that not better than always prospering, alone?

(N. Ngoc Bich, B. Raffel, and W. S. Merwin, *One Thousand Years of Vietnamese Poetry*, New York, Alfred A. Knopf, 1975)

Typically, natural flooding is relied upon in areas where land is cheap and plentiful. Here a farmer will sow seed by broadcasting it from a basket (see Plate 17), rather than placing a few seeds carefully into dibbling holes. Where broadcasting is used, a much greater area can be sown by a single farmer within the available time. If several varieties are sown on different plots and these ripen over a period of weeks, then the demand for workers at harvest can be spread out so that the labour of one family alone will suffice.

This is not to say that the life of the farmer who practises broadcasting is a carefree one. As with all other types of farming, what is needed most is accurate prediction of future weather conditions—in particular, when the floods will come. But it is not local rainfall that causes the plains to flood. More important is the rain that has fallen in the headwaters and mountains which may be many hundreds of miles away. The deltas of the Red (Hong) River, the Mekong, and the Yangtze, for example, used to be flooded with water that fell as rain and snow in Yunnan Province, South China, and Tibet. Now it is simple enough, in the twentieth century, to

42

17. Broadcasting rice, Thailand. (Reproduced with the permission of the Royal Thai Embassy, London)

give farmers accurate assessments of when they should expect their river to rise and flood. However, this sort of farming has existed in the region for hundreds of years, since times past when communications along a river's length were poor or non-existent and certainly not fast enough to help the small farmer. So local knowledge must have been built up from other signs. Trial and error has led to strategies that worked sufficiently well for populations to grow. The farmers broadcast their seed when local rainfall has been sufficient to wet the land they have prepared, and then wait for the waters to rise. If the floods do not come soon enough, they may have to sow again as continuing dry weather will have killed the germinating seedlings.

Local knowledge may sound at first like simple superstition. For example, along the Mentaya River of South Borneo, farmers transplant their rice when the moon is waning. But farmers know that tides are related to the moon's phases and that tides are highest during the full moon, with slightly lesser tides after the new moon. During this period, water drains off the flat lowland plain very slowly, backed up by the tide. This means a risk of flood waters too high for the young rice plants. So farmers choose a period when the risk is lower—during the waning moon.

Farmers must also have some idea of how deep the floods will be, as different varieties withstand flooding to different depths. If the waters rise too fast, a crop may be overtopped and drown. Then again, there are rice varieties with extremely fast-growing stems which can compete with the rising tide. *Kanlong Phnom* ('jump mountain-high') is a Cambodian floating rice variety that can grow 10–15 centimetres each day and thus keep ahead of the water. Floating rice is produced on land which becomes deeply flooded each year in Bangladesh, Burma, Vietnam, and around the Great Lake in Cambodia. The rice seed is sown before the waters rise. Then as the floods come, the rapid growth of the stems enables the tops of the plants to keep above the water-level: stems may grow as long as 5 metres (see Plate 18). As the waters recede, the long stems subside towards the ground where they are harvested. As so much energy is devoted to stem growth, yields are low.

No dry-land weeds compete with the rice but some aquatic plants may spread and cause losses. The water hyacinth, a floating plant related to the lily family, has beautiful lavender flowers and air-filled leaf-stalks. It can clog irrigation channels and spread rapidly across available open water, blocking out rice. The water hyacinth originated in Latin America but was favoured as an ornamental plant for ponds and lakes. It was taken to other continents where it 'escaped' beyond the garden wall to become a serious weed.

As more people move into an area and settlements are established, the pressure of population will mean that the value of land increases. Also, plots traditionally farmed by a family will be sub-

18. Floating rice, Thailand. The farmer is standing in his flooded rice-field. (Reproduced with the permission of the International Rice Research Institute, Manila)

divided by inheritance. Each young family will therefore have to find ways of earning a living from the smaller plots that become typical of an area. To do this, they will probably have to find more intensive ways of using the land—by planting fruit trees, by building bunds to hold back water on the land for longer periods, and by learning to irrigate artificially, lifting water to the fields from rivers and tanks during drier seasons (see Colour Plate 10). Water-buffaloes will be used to help prepare the land, while fertilizers and new seed varieties may be introduced and transplanting implemented (see Colour Plate 11).

Transplanting Rice

Transplanting rice is the practice that marks off rice from all other cereals and distinguishes eastern rice production. Where rice is grown in Europe and America, it is almost never transplanted as this requires abundant cheap labour. First, the rice seed is broadcast in a moist nursery bed. After a week, the seedlings are thick on the ground and 5–8 centimetres high. About 40 days from sowing, the seedlings are pulled out in bundles, stacked and protected with wet leaves, then transported to the wet, prepared paddy-field. After pruning roots and shoots, the seedlings are planted out in rows. The rice may stand nearly permanently flooded in the paddy-field or the plot may be allowed to drain and dry, perhaps to be flooded again before harvest.

Given the economic and social conditions of South-East Asia, where high population densities make every acre count and labour cheap, it seems likely that traditional rice farming and transplanting will continue to be common for decades to come. However, where hired labour is used and wages are rising, as in the Central Plains of Thailand and Central Luzon, transplanting is currently being replaced again by direct seeding of the rice.

Working in the rice fields is hard but it has to be done at the hottest time of the year, before the rains come. A popular song from Vietnam captures graphically the arduous task of rice planting:

In the heat of mid-day, I plough my field
My sweat falls drop by drop like rain on the ploughed earth
Oh, you who hold a full rice-bowl in your hands
Remember how much burning bitterness there is
In each tender and fragrant grain in your mouth!

On a lighter note, this Vietnamese nursery rhyme makes an artless but refreshing appeal for rain:

Sky! let the rain fall down
So that there's water to drink
So I can plough my field
Sky! let the rain fall down
So we can eat white rice
    and chopped aubergine!

Rice Ceremonies

Oxen draw the plough at the major ceremonies of flood-plain agriculture, such as the annual Royal Ploughing Ceremony, which is celebrated in similar style and pomp in Thailand and Cambodia.

The idea that a king should guide the plough goes back deep into South-East Asian myth and religion. In the *Ramayana*, for example, King Janaka was ploughing with a golden plough when he discovered a beautiful girl-child. He gave the child the name Sita, which means furrow, and later married her to Rama.

Again, sacred Buddhist texts of the Lesser Vehicle recount how the Buddha, as a baby, was left under the shade of a rose-apple tree whilst his father, the king, ploughed the ceremonial field. His nursemaids wished to see the gorgeous ceremony and left him for a moment. Their absence became prolonged and the sun rose in the sky. The nursemaids, shameful and fearful, finally ran back to the baby. They found, to their relief and astonishment, that the shadow of the tree had remained stationary to protect the child.

In May, the Japanese Emperor personally sets out rice in the grounds of his palace. In both Thailand and Cambodia, the Royal Ploughing Ceremony is a major public ceremony, marking the beginning of the rice-planting season and the new agricultural year. According to the old ways, the king is the Lord of the Flatness of the Earth. At the Ploughing Ceremony, he addresses higher beings in the hierarchy of gods and angels: Mae Thorani, Goddess of Vegetation; Phra Phum, Lord of the Earth; and Nag Megtala, who brings the rain.

In Thailand and Cambodia, it is no longer the king's hand that is required on the plough, but rather that of a 'Temporary Ploughing Lord' appointed for the ceremony—this may be the Minister of Agriculture. In both countries, the ceremony shows strong Brahmin influence and an auspicious day for it is set by Brahmin priests, who go on to lead the procession around the field. Some Buddhist elements have been added to the rites.

First, three folded lengths of handwoven cloth are presented to the Ploughing Lord and he must choose between them. If he chooses the longest, all is well as the length of the cloth symbolizes the forthcoming season's rainfall—the longest cloth indicates the highest rainfall.

At a signal from the deep-throated conch shells, ploughing commences. Three circles should be ploughed around the field. In Cambodia, three ploughs encircle the field—one guided by the Ploughing Lord, the other two by civil servants. The Ploughing Lord's wife, also ennobled for the day, broadcasts from her ornate container rice seed of the best variety and highest quality. The start of each circumambulation of the field is marked by another baying note from the conches.

19. 'Rabam Mae Posop'—traditional dance to render homage to the Rice Goddess. (Reproduced with the permission of the Oriental Hotel, Bangkok)

The sight is splendid: the oxen are white or golden-brown and bedecked with gold-and-red trappings and flowers (see Colour Plate 12). The Brahmins are dressed in fine white frock-coats edged in gold over white knee-length breeches and white socks. They chant and blow the conch shells, whilst drum- and umbrella-bearers in scarlet uniforms trimmed with gold follow after four beautifully attired, consecrated ladies of the court, who carry gold and silver baskets filled with rice seed.

After turning their furrows, the oxen are halted before a shrine set up for Lord Vishnu. They are unyoked whilst the head priest invokes the assistance of the gods for a good harvest. The oxen are sprinkled with lustral water and are then offered seven dishes of food and drink: rice, beans, maize, sesame, fresh grass, as well as water and alcohol. What the oxen choose is said to foretell prospects for the harvest. If they eat grain, then the harvest will be good; if they choose water, then the rains will be abundant and peace will reign, but should they choose alcohol, then thieves and bandits will proliferate in the land.

The Ploughing Lord then sprinkles rice in the furrows. After this, the press of daily reality rushes back to banish the mesmerizing ritual. Barriers which held back hundreds of farmers around the field are released and men and women run in to gather a few seeds from the ground to mix with their own crop seed, for good luck. Once the main ceremony has taken place, 'local' spirits and gods are invoked at village level in subsidiary events to celebrate the start of the new planting season. In the past, traditional dances would honour the Rice Goddess (see Plate 19).

The Water-Buffalo

Like the elephant, the water-buffalo is considered by the peoples of South-East Asia to have a soul. Indeed it is a very important animal, worthy of great consideration. The water-buffalo is clearly the main agricultural beast of burden in the flooded paddies—next in importance to women, who contribute up to 80 per cent of the human labour expended in South-East Asian rice farming.

In the amphibious agriculture of the South-East Asian flood

plains, what better animal could there be to share the farmer's burden? Domesticated 4,500 years ago, the water-buffalo is as happy to wallow in mud and rivers as it is to walk the land, unlike oxen and people who suffer assorted maladies in continually wet conditions. The characteristic that suits the water-buffalo to the role it plays in ploughing rice-fields is the size of its feet: its great splayed feet spread out its weight and thus enable it to walk on the muddy ground without causing damage or becoming stuck (see Colour Plate 13).

The natural habitat of the water-buffalo is the rain forest, where it can escape direct sunlight. In Thailand, water-buffaloes are captured or reared in the north of the country in areas that still have some forest cover, and they are then transported to the south and east to work for the farmers of the plains. This forest origin, however, means the water-buffalo is not well suited to working long hours in the sun: its skin is delicate and burns easily, and the animal is known to suffer sudden death from heatstroke if it is overworked. To avoid harming their animals, farmers will put them to the plough early in the morning and in the cool of the evening, and water is sprayed on them as they work. They are left to wallow in rivers and in mud during the hottest part of the day.

Valued for its usefulness and docility, the water-buffalo is also a powerful symbol across the region, representing wealth, status, and security. Buffaloes are frequently cared for and watched by children, who may ride on their backs. Buffaloes are expected to be gentle creatures—despite their formidable horns—and can be trusted.

Work in the rice-fields is hard—for man, woman, and beast. In Sumba, Indonesia, rituals are prescribed to protect the animal and also to make peace with it after ploughing. Village people keep their buffaloes in a corral outside the village, watched over by guardian spirits. As the rains approach, an offering is made to the spirits of the corral and the buffaloes are led down to the fields. The purpose of the offering is to speed the work of ploughing the fields by making the animals' hooves and the men's digging sticks sharper. Protection is sought for the female buffalo and her young. Once the rains are established, man and beast cross the field repeat-

50

edly, churning up the mud and destroying any remaining weeds. The work is arduous and is accomplished with beatings for the buffalo from cudgels and sticks. But once the work is done, another ceremony, called 'throwing away the cudgels', is held. This is intended to restore the previous good relationship between master and animal: sticks are left under banana plants and the buffaloes are returned to the cool and shade of their corral and given a ritual 'cooling of the hooves'.

For the Sumbanese, water-buffaloes are high-status livestock, as are horses. Cattle are seen mainly as economic animals to be bought and sold, but lacking any greater ritual significance. Water-buffalo bulls, especially those with very wide horns, may be worth up to ten times as much as ordinary buffaloes. The number of buffaloes slaughtered at a funeral is an indication of the importance of the deceased person (see Plate 20). Water-buffaloes are also slaughtered for meat once their working lives are behind them.

Water-buffaloes were once valuable at harvest time, when the large splayed feet proved ideally suited to threshing the newly gathered rice, separating the grain from the straw and chaff (see Plate 21). In the days when communities worked together at such tasks, competitions were arranged to thresh the village rice. The village buffaloes would be tied at intervals along a single rope attached to a stout post in the centre of the threshing floor. The animals would be encouraged to walk round the post, treading as they went the sheaves of rice laid out on the floor. Obviously, the buffalo at the outer end of the rope would have to trot round smartly, whilst those further in could walk much more slowly. Where a buffalo was lagging, it would be moved to a more central position which required less work. Once all the grain was threshed, the owner of the 'winning' buffalo—the one that had kept going longest—would be given a prize, often a length of cloth. After the event, the villagers would fill their baskets with grain.

A tale from the Philippines tells why the water-buffalo has a tightly fitting skin. One day, a black cow and a golden-skinned buffalo were working together in the fields. As the day grew hotter, they retired to a mud wallow where they each took off their

20. Buffalo horns fixed to the posts of a Toraja origin-house. (From
R. Waterson, *The Living House*, Singapore, Oxford University Press,
1990)

skin before launching themselves into the cool water and mud.
After some time, they heard the farmer approaching and, not
wanting to be found idling, they leaped back on to the bank and
put on their skins as quickly as possible. But unfortunately, they
each chose the wrong skin, which explains why the cow's skin is

21. Buffaloes threshing rice, Thailand (Reproduced with the permission of the Royal Thai Embassy, London)

so loose-fitting whilst that of the water-buffalo's fits so tightly across its body.

Another buffalo tale comes from Borneo. A rice-bird (*kandowei*) and a water-buffalo (*kerbau*) were drinking together at the bank of the river. The bird boasted to the buffalo that he could drink more water from the river than could the buffalo. The buffalo scoffed at this but the bird challenged him to a competition the next day. At the appointed hour, the buffalo began to drink, but soon noticed that not only was he not having any impact on the height of the water, but in fact, the water-level seemed to be rising. The buffalo stopped drinking, gasping that his stomach was full. The bird, who had cunningly timed the match for the moment at which the tide turns, then bent down and pretended to drink. Shortly afterwards it was clear that the water-level was indeed going down. Outwitted in this way by the rice-bird, the buffalo consented to become his slave, and so the bird is now to be seen riding on the back of the buffalo.

53

Although such stories suggest that the buffalo is a very stupid animal, it is nevertheless very much respected in South-East Asia and is looked upon as a symbol of security. The houses of many peoples across South-East Asia have wooden, crossed 'buffalo horns' set at either end of the roof. This form of decoration is common in northern Thailand, Sumatra, and Central Sulawesi. The horns may be finely carved or very simple but their purpose is the same—to protect the inhabitants of the house. In some places, a carved buffalo head may be added. This image is carried even further in Sumatra and northern Thailand, where the bulk of the house or a rice barn is likened to a buffalo body, with architectural features named after parts of the buffalo. There is a decorative board at a gable end called the buffalo's tongue and the lengthwise roof spars are called the stomach. In a northern Thai house, there was traditionally a lintel over the door to the sleeping-room intended to represent the genitalia of a male buffalo. This lintel symbolized power over evil and both protected the family and increased its fertility.

Minangkabau in West Sumatra is named after 'the buffalo's victory', and the following folk-tale describes how a young buffalo protected the people of Minangkabau 600 years ago when a new king of Java sent a message telling the people to surrender to him. The people of Minangkabau gathered to plan how they could keep their independence without the dangers of a battle. Eventually the people of West Sumatra proposed to the king of Java that the matter should be settled by a fight between two buffaloes. If the buffalo of the Javanese king won, they promised to surrender. If their own animal won, then the king must leave them in peace. The king agreed to this and put on to the battlefield an enormous buffalo such as had not been seen before. Large and powerful, it brought the people of West Sumatra near to despair. But one of the villagers had an idea to turn the tables. Taking a buffalo calf from its mother, they fitted its little horns with tips of iron, then waited for three days. On the next morning, the king's men brought the buffalo again to the battlefield and demanded to see his opponent. On came the buffalo calf, making the soldiers laugh.

The two animals looked each other over, then the calf ran towards the bull hoping to find milk—it had been kept from its mother for three days and was very hungry. The calf nuzzled the underside of the bull, but in doing so gored the bull with its sharp, iron-tipped horns. The bull gave a roar of pain and ran from the field, chased by the unsatisfied calf. The king left the battlefield quietly with his soldiers and his ambitions and was not seen again.

5
Mirroring the Sky

As the rice bows its head when it is heavy and ready for harvesting, so a wise man bends his head and is silent.

(Balinese saying)

Rice Terraces

ON steep hillsides, the narrow terraces gleam like sapphires or a broken mirror when the land has been recently tilled and water reflects the sky. As the growing season progresses, the transplanted rice starts to green the paddies with needle-thin shoots pointing up to the gathering clouds.

Terraced rice-fields are found in hilly and mountainous areas across South-East Asia—in Burma, Indonesia, and the Philippines. There are relics of prehistoric terraces in Vietnam and low valley terraces in Negri Sembilan, Malaysia. In gently rolling landscapes, the earth-retaining wall need be no more than a few metres high. As the hills become steeper, higher earth banks are capped with stone; in the mountains of northern Luzon, the Ifugao people have built stone walls that rise 6–15 metres upwards, carefully following the terrain. The terraces of Luzon (see Colour Plate 14), where so little else grows apart from grass and rice, are bleak in comparison with the lush terraces of Bali (see Colour Plate 15).

The terraces of the highland rice farmers represent their investment in the land over generations. If the terraces are poorly maintained and are allowed to slide downhill, a family's inheritance is lost. The original work of building the terraces was co-operative and their maintenance continues to be a communal effort. An individual's landholding tends to be small and is probably scattered in narrow plots across the hillside. A farmer has as urgent an interest in the strength of his neighbours' terrace walls as in that of his own. Where modern roads have been built, the delicate balance of a hillside has sometimes been lost and a hundred terraces have subsided towards the valley floor.

On South-East Asian terraces, the first farming operation is the ploughing of the freshly soaked field. Water is led from channels closely watched by all to ensure a fair distribution. All farmers in a locality will attempt to synchronize their activities. An individual who finds that surrounding farmers have harvested their crops before he does will suffer as pests concentrate on his land. Moreover, some farming activities are carried out by community groups to save on the labour needed. This can be important where a family wishes to farm more land than it has the labour to maintain. Pest control may also be carried out by a village as a whole in order to eradicate rats and other vermin from a wide area.

This folk-tale of rodent control comes from Central Java and explains why some snakes may be left unharmed. Dewi Sri (also known as the Rice Goddess) was the daughter of the Raja of Mataram, Lombok. She lived in Mendang Kauwlan, the capital city. The old Raja wished to retire, so he summoned his son Sudano and asked him to take the role of ruler. But Sudano was given more to meditation than to power and declined the offer, begging to be excused—he wished to be a hermit. The old Raja became angry and cursed his son, saying: 'Go then. But you go, not as a man but as a small rice-bird!'

Dewi Sri heard the commotion between her father and Sudano and came running in just in time to see a small *glatik* bird fly out of the window. She realized what had happened and begged the old Raja to bring back her brother, 'or I will follow him', she threatened. This incensed the Raja even more. He cried, 'All right, then, follow him. But you shall crawl as a snake.'

Next morning, a peasant found a python in his rice-field. As he raised his sickle to kill it, the snake spoke: 'I am Dewi Sri. Please do not kill me. If you let me live, I will promise you a rich harvest.' The peasant hurried to bring the python offerings of flowers and incense. He was rewarded with a bountiful harvest as the snake ate up all the rats and other pests.

At the turn of the present century, an anthropologist named Jenks wrote a patronizing account of the farming methods of the people of the central mountain zone of the Philippines. He scoffed at the local people's lack of knowledge of the scientific basis of their own farming techniques, though he could not deny that the techniques were effective. For example, the people pile earth in mounds in order to aerate it and so encourage any vegetation to decompose and provide nutrients for the coming crop; they also collect plant residues for spreading on the land as green manure. Pigs are kept in pigsties where they consume kitchen wastes, converting them to a stronger manure to be mixed into the soil of the terraces.

Bird-messengers and Bird-scarers

All farmers must judge carefully when to start the new season's farming activities but the Bontoc of Luzon face an additional threat. Luzon Island lies in the path of typhoons from the Pacific, which start to track in each year in May. The farmers must endeavour to plough early enough and harvest their crops before the typhoons strike. To ensure crops are planted in time (i.e. in October), the Bontoc have traditionally relied not on the stars but on a migratory bird, the *kiwing*, which regularly returns to Central Luzon in October. When these birds arrive, work begins; if there is any delay, the crop may be blasted by typhoons. Sometimes, even if the crop escapes the typhoons, the heavy rains of May may make the grain heads become sodden and virtually impossible to harvest. Colour Plate 16 shows a work-group transplanting rice on the Ifugao terraces in the Philippines.

Once the rice is ripening, birds are less welcome. Like all other rice-growing people, the Bontoc have developed a series of bird-scarers that employ great ingenuity to keep the birds from the crop, using local materials. The *kong-ok*, which is the horn of a water-buffalo cut at both ends to give a tube of 20 centimetres long, relies on sound. Boys beat on these horns when birds are near and the open, resonant sound can be heard a mile away. Another noisy device is shown in Figure 2. When the lower bamboo of this Dusun bird-scarer fills up with water from the

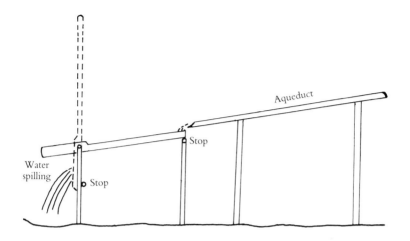

Fig. 2 Dusun bird-scarer, activated by water. (From O. Rutter, *The Pagans of North Borneo*, London, Hutchinson & Co., 1929; reprinted Singapore, Oxford University Press, 1985)

stream, it tips and bangs against the post. Then it empties and thumps back into place to be filled again.

A more complicated system makes use of the jerking movement of a piece of wood suspended in a stream. This movement is transferred by a series of cords that connect poles set in the fields. To the poles are tied lines strung out a metre or two above the rice. As the block of wood in the stream jerks in the current, the lines twitch over the rice. Systems like this, which use lines bedecked with scraps of fabric or leaves, are also prevalent in other parts of South-East Asia. In Borneo, for example, Kayans link tall, upright bamboos with rattans. The bamboos are placed at intervals of 20–30 metres across a field. Pulling on the rattans will set the bamboos moving across an area of almost half a hectare. Colour Plate 17 shows such a long-distance bird-scarer.

Then there is the Bontoc *ki-lao*—this is a basketwork figure swung on a pole, usually in the shape of the extended wings of a predatory bird, such as a gull, or it may be shaped like a man or lizard. The woven shape is attached to a 3-metre pole set in the ground at an angle so that the 'wings' hang free to be blown by the wind, about 1 metre over the growing grain. Where many are placed together over a field, they resemble a flock of restless birds and are very effective in keeping off the small brown rice-bird, the *ti-lin*.

A sad little tale is told of the origin of the rice-bird, the *ti-lin*. As a woman was pounding rice for supper, her little girl said, 'Give me some *mo-ting* (uncooked rice) to eat'. Her mother refused, saying it was not good till cooked. The little girl persisted until her mother told her to stop. Once the rice was pounded and cleaned, the woman went to fetch water. Whilst she was gone, the little girl reached for the basket of rice but the tray slipped and the girl was covered by rice and basket.

When the woman returned, she heard a bird crying 'king-king nik'. She lifted the basket and a little brown rice-bird flew away, calling 'Goodbye, mother, goodbye—you would not give me *mo-ting* to eat!'

Growing Rice on Bali

The hill-slopes of much of the island of Bali, down from a central spine of mountains, are clothed with terraces which reach up from the rice-fields of the plains like giant staircases towards the ridge. Closely ordered co-operation between farmers is necessary for the island's intensive use of both the land and the water provided by two central lakes. The Balinese have achieved this co-operation over a period dating from perhaps a thousand years ago.

As with all other Balinese institutions that involve communal interests, associations are set up allied to temples. Temples unite the three worlds of Bali: the upper world of gods, the realm of *maya* or illusion that is ours to inhabit, and the lower world of demons. A hierarchy of water-temples determines how a common resource can be shared to the benefit of all. Responsibility for the wise use of water resources passes from a mountain temple, down through *subak* temples to the local level or *tempek*, which covers a small group of farmers acting together. The temples are both ornate buildings and institutions of authority. They are animated by worshippers only once or twice a year when farmers bring offerings to the spirits who are said to reside there temporarily. All farmers, rich or poor, have access to water in proportion to their need.

The use of water from both the central lakes of Bali is controlled by two principal mountain water-temples. Pura Bata Kau controls water use in western Bali and Pura Ulun Danau controls the irrigation of paddy-fields elsewhere on the island. Downstream from the lakes are the channels through which water is conveyed to every scrap of irrigable land—through holes cut in rocks, along bamboo pipes, and along ditches. Controlling water use around each major channel is a mountain temple, which is responsible for perhaps a dozen subsidiary *subak* temples, each covering an area of about 80 hectares. The aim of the temple system is to regulate demand so that the need for water from the lakes remains more or less constant throughout the year. Demand for water would be very erratic if all farmers were to plant in the same month; indeed, this would synchronize peak demand for water for flooding the terraces. However, under the water-temple system, *tempek* groups agree to stagger their planting plans so that when one *tempek* area requires water for flooding, other groups will not clamour for it. By staggering planting seasons at the *tempek* level, the demand made by a higher-level *subak* temple can be kept more or less steady throughout the year. Then the requirements of the different *subak* areas are counterbalanced to ensure that the demand for water is constant within the area controlled by a mountain temple. Plate 22 shows part of the grounds of a Balinese water-temple.

The Balinese are Hindus and their legend of the origin of rice involves the rape of Mother Earth (the 'Smitten Grandmother') by Vishnu, Lord of the World. Indra, Lord of the Heavens, then taught men how to grow rice. Rice is not only the basic sustenance of the body, but also the soul of man, incorporating male and female creative forces, as earth and water both unite to give rice. It was also believed that Brahma (Sanghyang Kesuhum Kidul in Bali) gave rice to man, sending four doves with rice of three colours as well as the spice turmeric. These four colours (black, red, white,

61

22. A water-temple, Bali. The site of periodic ceremonies associated with rice growing, it is also the symbolic site for the organization of irrigation. (David Kinnersley)

and yellow) have come to be associated with the four cardinal points of the compass, with the north corresponding to the direction of the largest mountain in the locality and the south corresponding to that of the sea.

When a Balinese plants out the first clump of transplants into his rice-field (*sawah*), he does so in a prescribed order after offerings have been made to Dewi Sri, wife of Vishnu and Goddess of Rice. The first nine seedlings are planted as a square starting at the centre, then spiralling outwards in a clockwise direction. This pattern represents the magical Balinese rose of the winds (*nawa sanga*).

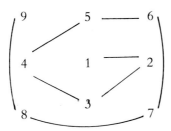

A series of rituals accompany each stage of rice farming, starting with the ritual of opening the water channel. Each of these stages is followed by an act of purification of the *sawah*: sprinkling on the field holy water which has been taken from the central lakes and blessed by the priests of the mountain temple. The rituals for the growing rice liken it to the life cycle of human beings: when the seeds are developing, the rice is said to be pregnant; then when they appear, a birth ritual is performed which includes 'singing to the baby rice'. Further rituals follow as the rice ripens, is harvested, and then stored in the barn. A Balinese rice granary is shown in Plate 23.

23. Balinese rice granary (*lumbung*). (Garth Sheldon, from R. Waterson, *The Living House*, Singapore, Oxford University Press, 1990)

Offerings to Balinese Gods

Visitors to Bali will be impressed by the offerings made to the gods at the many Balinese festivals. Layers of cooked and coloured rice cakes may be built up into a conical offering or *tumpeng* sometimes around 1.5 metres high. Usually, the elements of the offering are made by women, but the whole construction is assembled by men. Flowers and palm leaves decorate the offering which is carried on a silver tray. The decoration at the top of the pile will often be a *cili*, a female figure cut from palm leaves and representing Dewi Sri.

The *jaja* is another form of decoration used at Balinese festivals; it is made from brightly coloured rice paste shaped into many designs. *Jaja* may be geometrical, or shaped like people, or made to resemble the *cili* which is associated with Dewi Sri. These highly decorative biscuits are made in different ways. One type is made by steaming and pounding the rice, colouring it, and then rolling it into a rope of *kuluban* which is coiled into a spiral or pressed into a triangular, square, or rectangular mould. Another type of *jaja* known as *satuh* is made by frying rice without oil, then pounding it into a flour and adding palm sugar. The tasty but fragile *satuh jaja* are placed in delicate baskets of palm leaf plaited into designs resembling a bird or a mangosteen flower. *Jaja* may be tied together on strings to decorate a great piled offering of fruit and flowers or, for example at a Brahmin wedding, laid out in a display—a *sarad*—of demonic faces and doll-like figures (*deling*) around the central figure of Boma, a male god symbolizing fertility and plant life (see Colour Plate 18). *Jaja* decorate ceremonies that are both merry and solemn. The merit that accrues from these offerings does not derive from their size, but from the sincerity and thoughtfulness with which they are made.

A third type of Balinese offering is shown in Colour Plate 19: multicoloured cones of cooked rice are presented to recall the *nawa sanga* or rose of the winds.

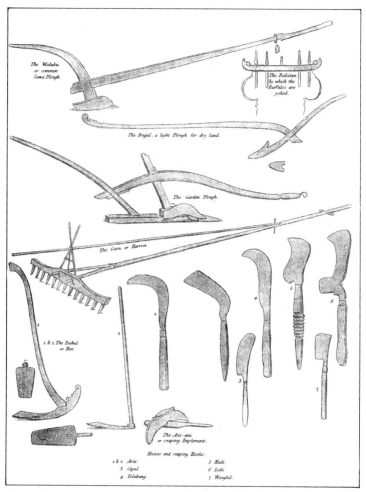

24. Implements used in traditional Javanese rice farming. (From T. S. Raffles, *The History of Java*, London, 1817; reprinted Kuala Lumpur, Oxford University Press, 1965 and 1978)

Ox Races

Plate 24 shows some of the agricultural implements used in Java in Raffles's day; some are still being used. The harrow, for example, has a subsidiary purpose. At planting time, bull races are held in northern Bali. The races are a way of getting the fields prepared, pleasing the gods with a fine spectacle, and having fun at the same time. Traditionally, the trained oxen wear ornaments of tooled and gilded leather, with silk banners attached to their yokes and bells to their necks. Bets are placed on the races and young men stand on the harrow hitched to a yoke. At a signal, the oxen set off across the field at a most unaccustomed pace, with their heads forced up by the weight of the bells, and pulling the harrows, which glide over the mud, carrying the young men. A referee eventually judges the outcome of the race, which goes not to the swiftest, but to the team with the most elegant bearing.

6
Rituals, Gods, and Legends

Rice in Ritual

As befits a crop which has been the mainstay of people for thousands of years, rice plays a significant role in many South-East Asian rituals. Cooked rice is offered to friends, to family, and to gods in many different ways: sometimes scented, sometimes coloured (either naturally or artificially), sometimes as rice wine or spirits. Not only is rice used to cement relationships and to enhance status, it is also used to make medicines and magic potions. As a paste, it often features in purification ceremonies.

Purification with rice occurs at ceremonies of all kinds in Malaysia and elsewhere in South-East Asia: at marriages and births, before building a house, before setting off on a major hunting expedition, or before starting the farming operations of the new season. Leaves from shrubs believed to have medicinal or magical properties are tied together with shredded tree bark to make a brush. The brush is fumigated with incense; then a thin rice paste is taken upon the brush and shaken out until almost dry (to avoid leaving tears of rice paste on the object to be purified). The object of the ceremony—a house, a weapon, or a child—is lightly brushed with the posy of leaves and twigs to bring about purification.

Ceremonial rice may take at least three forms. Rice parched by rapid heating in a pan, without oil, is spread over the bottom of sacrificial trays of offerings. 'Saffron' rice, which has been stained yellow with turmeric, is scattered on the people at the centre of a ceremony, such as the bride and bridegroom in a wedding. At sacrificial banquets, glutinous rice is served. Hulled, uncooked rice figures in Batak feasts in Sumatra: small handfuls are dropped on to the bowed heads of wife-receivers as a blessing by those who make the gift of wives.

Respect is accorded to rice at each of its various stages and men are usually not allowed to do such things as taking it from the granary or cooking it, unless there are no women in their family to do this. Women taking rice from the granary must show due deference. In eastern Indonesia, for example, a woman must observe certain rules: she must not enter the barn during times when the rice spirit might be sleeping (at night or noon); she must enter with her right foot first; and she must be properly dressed, with her breasts covered. She should not chew betel or talk whilst in the rice barn. Cooked rice must not be stepped over.

The reverence in which the rice seed is held by the Iban may be heard in the following prayer, which accompanies replanting:

Oh sacred padi,
You the opulent, you the distinguished,
Our padi of highest rank;
Oh sacred padi
Here, I am planting you:
Keep watch over your children
Keep watch over your people
Over the little ones, over the young ones.
Oh do not tire, do not fail in your duty.

Skeat, the authority on Malaysian magic, recounts the reaping ceremony he saw in Selangor, Malaysia. A mother-sheaf of fine, healthy, ripe rice was chosen within the field and, still standing, was encircled with a cord. Seven heads of rice were selected to be the 'rice child' and were cut with due ceremony and incense. These heads were then laid in a basket carried in a sling from a woman's neck and protected from the sun by a parasol. The rice child was taken to the farmer's house and laid on a sleeping mat with pillows at its head. For three days, certain taboos were observed, which are much the same as those surrounding the birth of a human child: perfect quiet was maintained and a light was placed near the head of the rice child and kept burning all night. No one's hair could be cut during this critical period.

Rather similar traditions exist across South-East Asia, with minor differences in the rituals—for example, differences in the stage at which the Rice Mother is selected for special treatment.

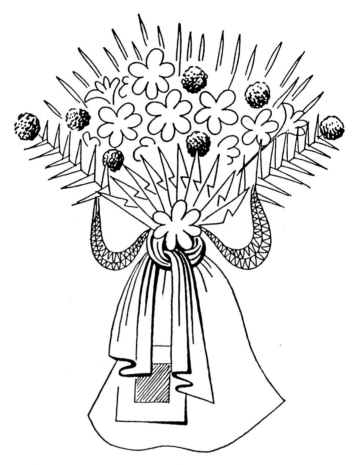

25. Balinese Rice Mother, made from a sheaf of rice. (From M. Covarrubias, *Island of Bali*, New York, Alfred A. Knopf Inc., 1937; reprinted Kuala Lumpur, Oxford University Press, 1972)

The common ground between all these rituals is that rice is to be well treated, protected, and honoured, lest it should fail and famine ensue. There are clear parallels in some of these traditions in far-away Europe—we can only wonder whether this is coincidence, or a common origin. Compare European corn dollies with the Balinese Rice Mother shown in Plate 25. The Balinese version is made from a sheaf of rice topped with a 'head-dress' of stalks decorated with flowers and sections of palm leaf shaped into a fan. The Rice Mother is dressed in a white skirt, an apron, and a silk scarf.

Customs for a Lifetime

Rice is an essential ingredient of the major ceremonies of a person's life in South-East Asia. A vital part of the wedding ceremony in parts of Malaysia is the *pokok nasi* (see Colour Plate 20), which is part of the *hantaran* custom of presenting gifts to a newly married couple. An artificial 'tree' is made of boiled eggs attached to leaves and stems which have been painted gold. The stems are then 'planted' in a bed of glutinous rice, coloured yellow with turmeric. The glutinous rice and the eggs and leaves are symbols of fertility. In Central Sumatra, rice is thrown over the bridegroom's head before he enters his bride's house, together with betel (*sirih*) leaves and lime. Later in the festivities, there is the custom of 'pulling the fried chicken under yellow rice'. A whole cooked chicken is buried under a cone-shaped heap of rice. The bride and groom have to seize either end of the chicken and attempt to pull it out at the same time. If the bride gets the thigh bones and the husband the head, then this indicates that in their new life, the husband will be master and protector of his family. Should the wife find herself holding the head, then it is said that the husband will be henpecked.

At the end of a wedding ceremony in Central Java, drinks and food are served and the bridal pair are presented with a specially decorated dish of yellow rice. The bridegroom takes a handful of rice which he kneads into a compact mass and gives to the bride. This ritual expresses the idea that the bride should be content with

71

everything the bridegroom possesses or earns, however little this may be.

Rice is also important at birth celebrations. In Perak, Malaysia, it was once customary to present a newborn child to the spirits of the river. On the fortieth day after birth, the child was carried to the river by a merry crowd of men and women taking offerings with them. These would include a quantity of parched rice, yellow rice, purifying rice-dust, and two coconuts, as well as a fowl, an egg from a black hen, and a quid of betel. In addition there would be seven long packets of cooked rice, seven square packets of cooked rice, a light vessel made of palm leaf, and a banana flower.

The offerings of rice packets, betel, and eggs were made at the riverside. The purifying rice-dust was sprinkled around like holy water, the parched and yellow rices scattered on the water. Finally, the vessel and banana flower were set adrift to float downstream, bearing away any possibility of lurking evil.

South-East Asian cultures are closely related with water and boats as well as with rice. When a new boat (*prahu*) is built in Indonesia, offerings are concealed within its keel. Rice is an essential ingredient of these offerings.

Rice Gods

In the spirit worlds of South-East Asia, there are many gods and goddesses associated with rice: those who gave rice to mankind; those who taught women to cultivate, harvest, and store it; and the rice spirits themselves. Colour Plate 21 shows a wooden image of the Rice God from the Philippines. Bok Sri—also known as Dewi Sri—is a Javanese rice spirit or goddess who unites with Djaka Sudana, the male spirit of the rice, in order to create a new harvest. Their union is celebrated with the full ceremonial of a marriage in the *slametan metik* ritual to which people working in nearby fields are invited. Invitations to the 'wedding' are issued very shortly before the ceremony. These 'witnesses' are an essential part of the ceremony but only men attend and eat, taking home with them the remains of the feast. Referred to as the *sri kawm* food tray, this leftover food is symbolic of the food a husband provides for his wife and family. The ritual identifies every wife with Bok Sri and every husband with Djaka Sudana, thereby reaffirming the state of marriage.

In Thailand, the Rice Goddess is Mae Posop. Mae Posop and the Balinese Rice Goddess, Dewi Sri, are treated in similar respectful and protective ways. Just as mothers give food and milk to their children to sustain them, so Mae Posop gives her body and soul to make the body of men and women. Indeed, it is the fact that man's diet consists of rice that sets him apart from the other animals.

The pregnant Rice Goddess is thought to crave bitter fruits (limes and lemons) and, as she is at the peak of her beauty, to enjoy admiring herself in a mirror. Offerings are carried to the fields by women as the Rice Goddess is shy and would be frightened away by men, which would ruin the crop. Colour Plate 22 shows a field shrine on which offerings to Dewi Sri are placed. No loud noises are made in the rice-fields, for fear that the rice may 'miscarry' and fail to yield. For the same reason, there is no talk of death or demons in the rice-field. When the rice ears begin to form, the rice plants are looked on as infants, and women go though the fields 'feeding' the flowering rice with rice pap, just as they would a baby. A more forceful approach is taken in Borneo, where a dance feast is given just after sowing, and masks are worn to frighten away both evil spirits and rodents (see Colour Plate 23).

At harvest time, it is traditional for Thai farmers to designate certain heads of rice as the Rice Mother. These are cut with a small knife concealed in the hand, so as not to scare the fearful rice spirit. Once this has been done, the rest of the rice can be cut with other implements, ready for a celebratory harvest dance (see Colour Plate 24). At one time, reapers in the field conversed in a special form of speech that would be unintelligible to the rice spirit, so that it had no warning of the impending harvest knife. When harvest comes, Mae Posop is thanked and her pardon asked for reaping the rice. The rice is cut and carried to the threshing floor. A woman goes back to the stubble and collects some of the fallen rice grains and places them in a little basket. She takes some straw and makes a doll from it (no more than the size of her hand). Settling it in among the rice grains, the woman calls to the rice soul to come and inhabit the doll. The basket is then carried back to the granary, where it is installed with ceremony.

The Thais call to Mae Posop, the Rice Mother, to bless their crops:

Oh Rice Goddess, come up into the rice bin,
do not go astray in the meadows and fields for mice to bite you and birds to take you in their beaks. Go to the happy place to rear your children and grandchildren in prosperity. Come!

If any rice should be spilt on the way back from the fields, an Iban farmer will whisper an apology. If—and this is worse—the rice falls into the mire under the longhouse and cannot be recovered, then a special ritual has to be observed to make amends. This involves throwing a piece of wood symbolizing a ladder under the house and pouring water over it to help the rice spirits find their way back up to the granary. Sometimes a cock is waved to propitiate the rice spirits, who are treated as though they were real people with a society of their own. All members of the rice family—whether they be hunting, fishing, or whatever—are implored to return to the farm and granary at the end of the harvest. A trail of puffed rice may be scattered to guide the rice spirits home.

To the Iban people of Sarawak, Pulang Gana is a spirit who presides over the earth and causes rice to grow. There are several stories describing the origin of Pulang Gana but all contain a common motif: early efforts to grow rice were unsuccessful and forest cleared of bush was reinstated overnight. Pulang Gana was asked to explain this and he replied the appropriate procedures had to be followed. These included making offerings of jars, bracelets, shells, ornamental shells, and glass beads before clearing land. Next, gifts of cooked rice and the ingredients of a betel chew were to be offered, as well as rice beer, and a hen's egg.

In a variant of this story, problems with rice production came later: one basket of rice seed planted would give only one basketful of grain at the end of the season. When the spirit was asked for advice, it enquired about the way in which the farmers addressed their parents-in-law. Told that the farmers simply used their given names, the spirit recommended that they speak more respectfully to their in-laws if they wished for better harvests.

A rather odd tale of the origin of rice comes from Vietnam. Once upon a time, the grain of rice was a very large ball. It did not need to be cultivated. At harvest time, people merely lit incense and candles and prayed, and the rice grain would come into their houses.

However, there was once a lazy wife. Her husband ordered her to sweep the floor clean in order to welcome the rice, but she kept procrastinating. The husband finished praying and the rice arrived sooner than expected. Startled and furious, the woman seized her broom and struck the unfortunate grain, which burst into a thousand fragments. From that day to this, and because of this misdemeanour, people must plant rice, harvest it, and pound it.

The stars and the heavens are also caught up in many tales about rice. The height of the Pleiades in the sky is a useful reminder to some peoples of whether planting time is approaching. The Klemantan of Borneo know the Pleiades as 'the Well', whilst the great square of Pegasus is called 'Palai'—the rice storehouse. The Klemantan recounted this traditional story to Charles Hose, who was travelling in Borneo at the beginning of the century. The constellation now known as Orion was, for the Klemantan, the representation of Laataang, a man who married the daughter of the constellation Pegasus. Laataang went to live in the sky but his marriage was doomed as his wife was ashamed of his crude farming methods. In particular, his left arm was cut off when he bungled an attempt to clear land for planting rice. (The Klemantan do not discern a 'left arm' to the Orion figure.) Eventually, dissatisfied with life in the sky, Laataang returned to live on Earth, but he brought sugar-cane and banana with him from the heavens.

Rain Gods

At the start of the farming year, the first ploughed furrow must be pointed in the right direction, so as not to ruffle the scales of the great world serpent, the Naga, which rotates its position through the seasons. A farmer should ask the local guardian spirit of the earth for permission to clear the brush and stab the earth with a plough.

Farmers everywhere supplicate the gods and spirits for their intercession with the harvest: to make the rains come on time and in sufficient quantity and to make them stop when the rice is ripe so that it can be harvested and stored. Whilst rice is in the fields, farmers may plead for help with controlling rodents and other pests.

Sympathetic magic has been used to attract the Rain God's attention to the farmers' pleas. In the 1880s, for example, a ceremony was recorded that involved two men thrashing each other with rods until blood ran down their backs like the water they wanted to receive. Cats also feature in appeals for rain. Malay women have been known to wash cats in earthenware bowls, whilst in Thailand a cat (Nang Maew) may be carried through the streets of small towns in a basket and householders invited to throw water on the cat. The hullabaloo created by the cat and the merry villagers is intended to wake the Rain God: 'Hail Nang Maew! Give us rain, give us holy water to pour on Nang Maew's head.'

Another tactic to attract rainfall used in the last century was to invite the golden toad in from his swamp to attend a recitation of holy writings: the golden toad is taken to be an incarnation of a Bodhisattva. In other cases, a Buddha image is taken from a shrine to a place where people throw water at each other to encourage clouds to release their rain. An old Burmese rite brings two teams to a tug of war. This stems from the belief that the Burmese spirits, or *nat*, are very fond of battles, especially mock battles, and will join in the tug of war with thunder and lightning.

Rockets are a common way of attracting the attention of celestial beings. In Burma and Thailand, these rockets are set off at the time of year when rain might be expected. The height of the highest rocket is meant to indicate the amount of rain to be expected: if the rockets fly high, the rain and therefore the harvest will be abundant. Anthropologists have suggested the rocket is a phallic symbol, reminding the male Rain God to fertilize Mother Earth. An alternative approach, recorded from Thailand, involves the use of clay figures copulating in the rice-fields—the idea behind this is that the gods will be offended by such sights and will attempt to wash them away with rain. Calling and commanding the Rain God was another method used, but this entails the risk of the caller being struck by lightning.

Once enough rain has fallen, the entreaties to the gods are that the rain should stop and the floods subside. The Tonle Sap in Cambodia is one of the very few rivers in the world that run in two directions, depending on the time of year. When the Mekong is in flood, the Tonle Sap flows towards the Great Lake, but as the water begins to ebb, it reverses its flow and moves towards the sea. In order to 'ensure' that this change of flow occurred at the right time, canoe races in which the king and his court took part were organized on the river.

The Chao Phraya, which flows from northern Thailand past the old capital of Ayutthaya and through Bangkok, is tidal in its lower reaches. In the ancient kingdom of Ayutthaya, once harvest time approached, the Siamese kings would set out to the centre of the river and, with a golden sword, smite its surface three times to make it ebb.

Conclusion

Clearly, the old ways and the old customs are fading—some may say, even dying—in South-East Asia. Where dances and rituals are retained, it may be as much for the sake of the tourist industry as for any confidence in their effectiveness. There is no doubt that for many years there have been people who have looked with scepticism on traditional rites, but who nevertheless enjoy taking part in and honouring such customs. There are also probably some who participate 'just in case ...'.

Still there is value in recording and describing these customs: they are rich and detailed, reflecting the interplay of man's imagination and the natural world. The world will indeed be impoverished when they are lost. Not only do the common threads of the traditional beliefs present a means of tracing the spread of cultures and peoples but they also offer a tantalizing glimpse of ancient links within South-East Asia and with other parts of the world.

Select Bibliography

Anon., *Le chant du riz pilé*, Paris, Les Editeurs Francais Reunis, 1974.

Bray, F., *The Rice Economies: Technology and Development in Asian Societies*, Oxford, Basil Blackwell, 1986.

Brinkgreve, F. and Stuart-Fox, D., *Offerings: The Ritual Art of Bali*, Jakarta, Image Network Indonesia, 1992.

Chin, L., *Cultural Heritage of Sarawak*, Kuching, Sarawak Museum, 1980.

Covarrubias, M., *Island of Bali*, 1937; reprinted Kuala Lumpur, Oxford University Press, 1972 and Singapore, Oxford University Press, 1987.

Freeman, J. D., *Iban Agriculture: A Report on the Shifting Cultivation of Hill Rice by the Iban of Sarawak*, London, HMSO, 1955.

Grist, D. H., *Rice*, London, Longmans, 4th edn., 1965.

Matras-Troubetzkoy, J., *Un village en forêt: l'essartage chez les Brou du Cambodge*, Paris, SELAF, 1983.

Purseglove, J. W., *Tropical Crops: Monocotyledons*, 2 vols., London, Longman, 1972.

Roth, H. Ling, *The Natives of Sarawak and British North Borneo*, 2 vols., London, Truslove & Hanson, 1896; reprinted Kuala Lumpur, University of Malaya Press, 1968.

Skeat, W. W., *Malay Magic: An Introduction to the Folklore and Popular Religion of the Malay Peninsula*, London, 1900; reprinted Singapore, Oxford University Press, 1984.

Stott, P. A., *Nature and Man in South East Asia*, London, School of Oriental and African Studies, 1978.

Sutlive, V., *The Iban of Sarawak*, Prospect Heights, Illinois, Waveland Press, 1988.

Waterson, R., *The Living House: An Anthropology of Architecture in South-East Asia*, Singapore, Oxford University Press, 1990.

Zohary, D. and Hopf, M., *Domestication of Plants in the Old World*, Oxford, Clarendon Press, 1988.

Index

References in brackets refer to Plate numbers; those in brackets and italics to Colour Plate numbers.